AF307593

Marx Hardy Machiavelli Chesterton Cooper Emerson Joyce Austen
Abbott Defoe Melville Montaigne Haggard Hugo Grimm
Stoker Carroll Christie Maupassant Byron Eliot Molière
Wilde Garnett Einstein Fitzgerald Engels Schiller
Goethe Hawthorne Smith Kafka Hall
Cotton Dostoyevsky Willis
Baum Kipling Doyle
Henry Nietzsche
Leslie Dumas Flaubert Turgenev Balzac
Stockton Vatsyayana Crane
Burroughs Verne
Curtis Tocqueville Vinci
Homer Widger Tolstoy Whitman Gogol Busch
Darwin Thoreau Twain
Potter Freud Zola Lawrence Scott Harte
Kant Jowett Stevenson Dickens Plato
Andersen Burton Hesse
London Descartes Cervantes
Poe Aristotle Wells Voltaire
Hale James Hastings Cooke
Bunner Shakespeare Irving
Richter Chambers da Shaw
Doré Dante Chekhov Wodehouse Benedict Alcott
Swift Pushkin Newton

Wilmot and Tilley

James Hannay

Imprint

This book is part of TREDITION CLASSICS

Author: James Hannay
Cover design: Buchgut, Berlin – Germany

Publisher: tredition GmbH, Hamburg - Germany
ISBN: 978-3-8472-2114-2

www.tredition.com
www.tredition.de

THE MAKERS OF CANADA

EDITED BY

DUNCAN CAMPBELL SCOTT, F.R.S.C.,
PELHAM EDGAR, Ph.D., and,
WILLIAM DAWSON LE SUEUR, B.A., LL.D., F.R.S.C.

THE MAKERS OF CANADA

WILMOT AND TILLEY

BY
JAMES HANNAY

EDITION DE LUXE

TORONTO
MORANG & CO., LIMITED
1907

*Entered according to Act of the Parliament of Canada in the year 1907
by Morang & Co., Limited, in the Department of Agriculture*

Transcriber's Note: Unique page headings have been retained and appear along the left margin by the relevant paragraphs. Minor typographical errors have been corrected without note. Variant spellings have been retained. Inconsistent hyphenation has been standardised.

[ix]

LEMUEL ALLAN WILMOT

CHAPTER I

ANCESTRY AND EARLY LIFE

The contest for responsible government which was carried on in all the provinces of British North America for so many years resembled in some of its features a modern battle, where the field of operations is so wide that it is impossible for a general to cover it with his eye or to keep control of all the movements of his subordinates. In such a case, everything depends on the ability of the generals who command the different army corps, who, operating in remote parts of the field, must take the responsibility of success or failure. The two Canadas were so far removed from New Brunswick, and the means of communication were so poor, that there was but little help, even in the way of suggestion, to be expected from them, while the contest for responsible government was being carried on. Even the efforts in the same direction which were being made in the province of Nova Scotia had but little influence on the course of events in New Brunswick, for each province had its own particular grievances and its own separate interests. Thus it happened that the battle for responsible government in New Brunswick was fought, to a large extent, without reference to [2] what was being done in the other provinces which now form the Dominion of Canada, and the leaders of the movement had to be guided by the peculiar local circumstances of the situation. Still, there is no doubt that the efforts of all the provinces, directed to the same ends, were mutually helpful and made the victory more easily won.

Among the men who took a part in the contest for responsible government in New Brunswick, Lemuel Allan Wilmot undoubtedly held the foremost place, not only by reason of the ability with which he advocated the cause, but from the trust which the people had in him, which made him a natural leader and the proper exponent of their views. There were, indeed, men working in the same field before his time, but it was his happy fortune to witness the fruit of his labours to give the province a better form of government, and to bring its constitution into line with the system which prevailed in the mother country. He not only viewed the land of promise from afar, but he entered into it, and he became the first native lieuten-ant-governor of the province, — a result which even he, sanguine as he was, could hardly have contemplated when he began his career as a public man.

THE WILMOT FAMILY

Lemuel Allan Wilmot was born in the county of Sunbury, on the banks of the St. John River, on January 31st, 1809. He was the son of William [3] Wilmot, a respectable merchant and lumberman, who was in partnership with William Peters, grandfather of Sir Leonard Tilley. William Wilmot was the son of Lemuel Wilmot, a Loyalist, who was a resident of Poughkeepsie, New York, at the beginning of the Revolution. He (Lemuel) raised a company of soldiers for the service of the king, and became a captain in the Loyal American Regiment which was commanded by Beverley Robinson, serving in that corps during the war. At the peace, he came to New Brunswick and settled in Sunbury County on the river St. John. The Wilmots were a respectable English family, and the first of the name in America was Benjamin Wilmot, who was born in England in 1589 and came to America with his wife Ann, probably prior to 1640. He was one of the early settlers of New Haven, Connecticut, and the records of that colony show that he took the oaths of fidelity at a court held on May 2d, 1648. He died in 1669. His son William, who was born in 1632, was probably also a native of England. He mar-ried Sarah Thomas in 1658, and died in 1689.

Thomas Wilmot, his son, was born in 1679. He married Mary Lines, and their son Ezekiel was born in 1708. Ezekiel Wilmot and his wife Beulah were the parents of Lemuel, who was born in 1743. Lemuel Wilmot married Elizabeth Street, and William, the father of the subject of this biography, was their son. William Wilmot mar-ried Hannah [4] Bliss, a daughter of the Hon. Daniel Bliss, a Massa-chusetts Loyalist, who became a member of the council of New Brunswick and was the father of John Murray Bliss, one of the judg-es of the supreme court of that province. His grandfather was Colo-nel John Murray, a Massachusetts Loyalist, who was for many years a member of the general court of that colony and who became a mandamus councillor. It will thus be seen that Lemuel Wilmot came from the best New England stock, and that his connections were highly respectable and even distinguished. He was proud of his New England descent, and claimed the usual ancestor from among the passengers of the *Mayflower* who landed at Plymouth in 1620. If this claim is correct, his descent from the Pilgrim Fathers must have been through the female line, and no record of it has been preserved. The matter is not of much consequence at the present day, for the Wilmots have made a record in their province far more distinguished than that which they won in New England, for they have given to New Brunswick five members of the legislature, a senator and member of the House of Commons of Canada, two members of the executive of New Brunswick, and one of the privy council of Canada, an attorney-general and a provincial secretary of New Brunswick and two lieutenant-governors.

LIEUTENANT-GOVERNOR CARLETON

The system of government which existed in all the British North American colonies at the time [5] when L. A. Wilmot was born was practically the same. New Brunswick had been separated from Nova Scotia in 1784, and, in the autumn of that year, its first governor was sent out in the person of Thomas Carleton, a brother of Sir Guy Carleton. Thomas Carleton had been an officer in one of the regiments which fought during the War of the Revolution, but he was in no way distinguished, and had no special qualifications for the position he was called upon to fill. That fact, however, did not concern the persons in England who appointed him. In those days, fitness or ability had very little to do with colonial appointments. Carleton continued to fill the office of governor and lieutenant-governor until his death in 1817; but for the last fourteen years of his term he resided in England, and the duties of his office were performed by a succession of administrators under the name of presidents. To assist him in his deliberations, Carleton had a council of twelve members, who were appointed by the Crown and were therefore wholly under the influence of the governor and the authorities in England. In 1809, its number had been reduced to ten, and it was composed of the four judges of the supreme court, the provincial secretary and the surveyor-general, who held their offices for life, and four other persons. This council, in addition to its executive functions, also sat as the upper branch of the legislature, and, besides being wholly irresponsible except to the governor, it sat with closed doors, [6] so that the public had no opportunity of knowing what was being done. It was not until the year 1833 that any portion of the journals of the legislative council was published.

The House of Assembly consisted of members chosen by the freeholders of the several counties and the freeholders and freemen of the city of St. John. This House was able to exert but a limited influence on the government of the country, for all authority was vested in the lieutenant-governor and he was able to act in a manner quite independent of the legislature. All the appointments to office were in his hands, and they were made in many cases even without the knowledge of his council. In England, even under the most despotic kings, parliament was always able to curb the power of the Crown by refusing to grant supplies; but this check did not exist in New Brunswick, or in the other colonies of British North America at that time, because the governor had sources of revenue quite independent of the legislature. The British government maintained a customs establishment in the colonies, which levied duties on all merchandise imported, and over which the legislature had no control. The British government also retained the revenues arising from the Crown lands of the province, and these revenues the governor expended as he pleased. The House of Assembly, therefore, might refuse to vote supplies; but the governor could go on without them, and the only effect of such a procedure was [7] to injure its own officials, and to deprive the people of the money which was expended on roads and bridges.

THE CHURCH OF ENGLAND

Another feature of the system of government in New Brunswick was the predominant influence it gave to the members of the Church of England. Every member of the council of the province belonged to that denomination, and it was not until the year 1817 that any person who was not an adherent of the Church of England was appointed to the council. This exception was William Pagan, a member of the Church of Scotland, and his was a solitary instance because up to the year 1833, when the old council was abolished, all its other members were adherents of the Church of England. The same rule prevailed with respect to all the great offices in the gift of the Crown. All the judges of the supreme court for the first sixty-seven years of the existence of the province were members of the Church of England. L. A. Wilmot, who became attorney-general in 1848, was the first person not a member of the Church of England who filled that office, and he was the first judge not a member of that Church who sat on the bench of New Brunswick.

For some time after the foundation of the province, the salaries of the Church of England clergymen were paid by the British government, and large grants of land were made for the purpose of supporting the churches. In addition to this, financial [8] assistance was given to them in erecting their places of worship. No dissenting minister was allowed to perform the marriage ceremony, that privilege being confined to clergymen of the Church of England, the Church of Scotland, the Quakers and the Church of Rome. This was felt to be a very serious grievance, and, needless to say, produced a great deal of inconvenience.

Another grievance was the fact that the great offices were held by members of certain favoured families. These families, from their social position and in some cases from their wealth, had the ear of the governor, or of the authorities in England, and were able to obtain and hold all the valuable places. The two Odells, father and son, held the office of provincial secretary for sixty years. The Chipmans were another favoured family, both the father and son being successively judges of the supreme court, and the former receiving large sums from the British government as one of the commissioners who settled the boundary between Maine and New Brunswick. One of the greatest offices in the province—that of the surveyor-general—was held by one person for thirty-three years, and this individual was in no sense responsible to any authority in New Brunswick except the governor. Those in power at that day were very fond of expatiating on the glories of the British constitution and the privileges the people enjoyed under it. But nothing less like the British constitution can be imagined than [9] the system which then prevailed in the British North American colonies.

THE OFFICIAL CLASSES

One feature which is not to be lost sight of in considering the political condition of the province at that time is the social element. The distinctions between the upper classes and others was then far more marked than it is at present. The officials and the professional men formed a class by themselves, and looked with contempt upon those who were engaged in business. The salaries of the government officials were then three or four times as large as they are at present, and they kept up a corresponding degree of state which others were not in a position to imitate. This assumption of superiority was carried out in all the relations of life, and the sons of those who occupied an inferior station were made to feel their position keenly. This was the case with Lemuel Allan Wilmot, for, although his family was as good as any in the provinces, he was the son of a man who was engaged in business and who was not only a Dissenter but was actually a preacher in the denomination to which he belonged. No doubt the insults which the son received from those who claimed to occupy a higher station had a good deal to do with his zeal for the cause of Reform, and influenced his future career to a considerable extent.

William Wilmot, although he afterwards failed in business, was in prosperous circumstances when his son Lemuel was born. He was a Baptist and [10] was one of the original members of the Baptist Church at Canning, in Queens County, which was founded in 1800. On Christmas Day, 1813, William Wilmot and nine others received their dismissal from the Canning Church for the purpose of founding a Baptist Church in Fredericton. Wilmot was a local preacher and used his gift of eloquence in that way. He also aspired to legislative distinction, and was elected a member of the House of Assembly for the county of Sunbury in 1816. He was an unsuccessful candidate for the same seat in 1819, and again in 1820. At the general election of 1827 he ran for the county of York, to which he had removed several years before, but was again defeated. This was his last attempt to become a member of the House of Assembly. His loss of three elections out of four had certainly been discouraging, and was in singular contrast to the fortune of his distinguished son, who never experienced a defeat.

AS A LAW STUDENT

Lemuel Wilmot's mother died when he was only eighteen months old, so that he never knew a mother's love or a mother's care. But his father early recognized his youthful promise, and gave him all the educational advantages then available. He became a pupil at the College of New Brunswick, which was situated in Fredericton, of which the Rev. Dr. Somerville was the president and sole professor. This college was in fact merely a grammar school, but Wilmot acquired there some [11] knowledge of the classics. However, his scholastic career was not prolonged, for in June, 1825, he entered as a student-at-law with Charles S. Putnam, a leading barrister of Fredericton. He was admitted an attorney of the supreme court in July, 1830, and a barrister two years later. He was then twenty-three years of age.

The men who were contemporaries of Mr. Wilmot as a youth are all dead, and not many anecdotes of his career as a student have been handed down to us. Being of an ardent and ambitious disposition, he took a keen interest in the stirring events that were being enacted around him; for it was a time of great political excitement, and the business troubles of the province increased the difficulties of its inhabitants. In 1825, all the lumbermen in the province were ruined, and the bad management of the Crown lands office which had added to the business difficulties became more than a political question, for by cramping its leading industry it affected the prosperity of every man in New Brunswick. It was then that young Wilmot resolved to enter upon a political career and to do what he could to redress the wrongs from which the people were suffering. Strange to say, at this time he, who afterwards became most eloquent, had an impediment in his speech, which it took much labour to overcome. To improve his knowledge of French, he spent some months with a French family in Madawaska, among the descendants [12] of the ancient Acadians. In this way he acquired a colloquial knowledge of that language.

Wilmot's ambition was to become a public man and to assist in the reformation of the constitution of his native province. He enjoyed many advantages for the rôle he had undertaken. He was tall, his height being upwards of six feet, well proportioned, handsome and striking in his features, and he possessed a voice of great strength and sweetness. He was proficient in all athletic exercises, and took an interest in all those movements which commend themselves to young men of enterprise and force of character. He was a lieutenant in the first battalion of the York County Militia when he was only eighteen years of age, and his devotion to the militia force continued until the end of his life. Possessed as he was of all the elements which make men popular and prominent, he was early marked for advancement in the field that he had chosen for the exercise of his talents.

[13]

CHAPTER II
EARLY EFFORTS FOR REFORM

The agitation for an improvement in the constitution of New Brunswick began long before L. A. Wilmot was born. The first man who took a prominent stand for reform in the legislature was Mr. James Glenie, a member for the county of Sunbury from 1792 to 1809. Mr. Glenie, who was a Scotchman and a man of much ability, had been an officer in the Royal Engineers during the Revolutionary War. His efforts to obtain reforms were met by the friends of the governor, Mr. Carleton, with the most violent opposition. He was denounced as an incendiary, and indeed there was hardly a limit to the fierceness with which he was attacked for attempting to bring about an improvement in the system of government. The old Family Compact and their friends were ever ready to tell the public how loyal they were, and to denounce as a traitor any person who presumed to object to the existing state of things. Mr. Glenie was not able to effect anything substantial for the improvement of the constitution, because the time was not ripe for the changes he proposed. England itself was suffering at that time from a relapse from true constitutional methods, so it was not to be expected [14] that much attention would be paid to complaints which came from a remote province of North America.

The cause of Reform would not have been nearly so well supported as it was, had it not been for the fact that the abuses which existed touched the self-interest of many persons who were by no means Reformers at heart, and who in fact cared nothing about responsible government. The first successful attack which was made on the existing order of things was with regard to the fees charged on land grants. These fees went to the various officials, including the governor, and it was shown that on a lot of land not exceeding three hundred acres, the enormous sum of forty-seven dollars was charged as fees, while on a lot of one thousand acres to ten grantees, the fees amounted to about two hundred dollars. The reader will be able to understand from these figures how it was that the officials of the government were able to live in such princely style. This evil was remedied by permission being obtained from the colonial secretary to include a large number of grantees in one grant.

THE MARRIAGE QUESTION

Another grievance which was attacked long before Mr. Wilmot entered public life was the law which related to the performance of the marriage ceremony. At that time the only clerical persons authorized to solemnize marriages were the clergymen of the Church of England, ministers of the Kirk of Scotland, Quakers, and priests of the [15] Roman Catholic Church. This was felt to be an intolerable grievance, because it prevented Methodists, Baptists and all Presbyterians except those connected with the Church of Scotland from being married by their own ministers. In 1821 a bill was passed in the House of Assembly authorizing all ministers of the Gospel to solemnize marriages. This was rejected by the council, a fate which befell many subsequent bills of the same kind. For several years the House of Assembly continued to pass the Dissenters' Marriage Bill, and the council as steadily rejected it. Finally, in 1831, the House of Assembly concluded that nothing would serve to bring about the reform asked for but a petition to the king, and accordingly a petition was prepared in which the facts were set forth and His Majesty was asked to give instructions to the administrator of the government to recommend the legislature to pass a bill extending the privilege of solemnizing marriages to all regularly ordained clergymen of dissenting congregations in New Brunswick. In 1832, a bill was passed by both Houses carrying out these views. It contained a suspending clause, however, which prevented it from going into operation until approved by His Majesty. It was thought that this would settle the question, but in 1834 a despatch was received from His Majesty's secretary of state for the colonies in which it was announced that the royal assent had been withheld on the ground that the Act was [16] confined in its operation to four denominations of Christians,—the Wesleyan Methodists, the Baptists, the Presbyterian seceders from the Church of Scotland, and the Independents. It appeared, therefore, that the Act had been disallowed because it was not liberal enough, but this defect was speedily remedied by the passage of another bill during the session of 1834 in the terms suggested by the colonial secretary, and the Dissenters' Marriage Question was thus settled.

IMPERIAL CUSTOM DUTIES

It has already been stated that the British government continued to maintain a custom-house establishment in New Brunswick, and to impose duties on goods imported into the province. These duties, which were levied for the regulation of trade, were disposed of by the British government and by the lieutenant-governor of the province with little reference to the wishes of the legislature. The old restrictive system which placed shackles on trade was modified by two Acts passed by the imperial parliament in 1822, under which the importation of provisions, lumber, cattle, tobacco and other articles from any foreign country in North and South America and the West Indies, into ports of British North America and the British West Indies, was allowed under a fixed scale of duty, and a free export was allowed to goods going from all our ports to these countries. The importation of the productions of foreign countries in Europe into the ports of British North America was also [17] permitted, and a schedule of duties annexed. Under these Acts it was provided that the duties on both imports and exports were to be collected by the imperial officers of customs, and the net revenue thus obtained was to be placed at the disposal of the colonial treasuries. This arrangement was a decided gain to New Brunswick, because, for the first time, it placed nearly all the revenue collected by the imperial officers under the control of the legislature.

The Acts of the imperial parliament, 6th George IV, Chapters 73 and 114, went still farther in the way of removing restrictions from colonial trade. These Acts provided that the duties imposed under them should be paid by the collector of customs into the hands of the treasurer or receiver-general of the colony, to be applied to such uses as were directed by the local legislature of such colony, exception being made in regard to the produce of duties payable to His Majesty, under any Act passed prior to the eighteenth year of his late Majesty, George III. This exception is important for the purpose of illustrating the pernicious system under which duties had been collected. Even so late as the year 1833, Messrs. Simonds and Chandler, the New Brunswick delegates to the imperial government, were complaining that duties were collected at the several custom-houses in New Brunswick upon wine, molasses, coffee and pimento under the provisions of the Acts of parliament, 6th George II, [18] Chapter 13; 4th George III, Chapter 15, and 6th George III, Chapter

52, amounting to upwards of one thousand pounds sterling annually, which duties were not accounted for to the legislature, and that it was not known to the House of Assembly by whom and to what purpose these duties were applied. The reply to this on the part of the imperial government was, that in pursuance of the directions contained in the statutes themselves, the duties levied under them were remitted to the exchequer in England in aid of the expenses incurred for the defence of the British colonies in North America. Thus ten years after the British government had undertaken to remit the duties collected in the colonies to the exchequers of the colonies in which the money was collected, there still remained a considerable revenue, obtained under old and obscure Acts of parliament, which was held back, and the destination of which was not known, until disclosed to the delegates sent to England to obtain the redress of New Brunswick's grievances.

But the grievance which caused the greatest amount of dissatisfaction in New Brunswick was that which arose from the management of the Crown lands. It was bad enough that the revenues arising from the public domain should be disposed of without the consent of the legislature; but it was still worse when such regulations were made by the surveyor-general as hindered the settlement of the country and interfered with one of its leading industries. [19] One great abuse was that large areas of the best land in the province were locked up as reserves for the production of masts for His Majesty's navy. Another grievance was the imposition of a duty of a shilling a ton on all pine timber cut in the province. This was done by the authority of the surveyor-general, and its effect was seriously to injure many of those who were engaged in lumbering. This tax was remitted for a time after the panic of the year 1825, but it was revived when that crisis in the commercial life of the province had passed. The management of the Crown lands office had been the subject of criticism at almost every session of the legislature for twelve or fifteen years before Lemuel Wilmot entered public life, and every year the complaints grew louder.

AN ADDRESS TO THE KING

At the session of 1831, an address was presented to the president, the Hon. William Black, asking him to lay before the House a detailed account showing the amount of the casual and territorial revenue from the beginning of 1824 to the end of 1830, and the expenditures from that fund for the same period. This was refused on the ground that it was inconsistent with his instructions. The House then resolved to bring the matter to the notice of the king in an address, the spirit of which may be gathered from the following paragraphs: —

"By the operation of the system practised in this office, very large sums are taken from the people of this province for licenses to cut timber on Crown [20] land, and, although the assembly do not question the right Your Majesty undoubtedly has to the lands in question, they think the tremendous powers with which the commissioner is vested, with regard to impositions of tonnage money and the enormous exactions for fees, to be incompatible with a free government, and to require redress.

"It is generally understood, as well as universally believed, that the commissioner in question is under no control in this province, and to this may be ascribed the mode in which licenses to cut timber are issued in very many cases, in quantities less than one hundred tons, subject to a duty of one shilling, three pence per ton, and the excessive fee on each of forty-five shillings. By this mode, a large part of the receipts is paid in the shape of fees, at once injuring the subject without benefiting the revenue; and the assembly feel convinced, if the office were under colonial management, that while the oppressions would be removed, the revenue would be more productive; and besides, the assembly cannot but view with just alarm that the day may possibly come when, by a single mandate from the office, exactions of such magnitude may be made as literally to stop the export trade of the country, a power which no person should have even the shadow of authority to exercise.

"The assembly at an early day in the present session, by an address to the administrator of the government, sought for documents regarding this [21] office, to enable them officially to bring the subject more in detail under the consideration of Your Majesty, but this information, so highly desirable and necessary, has been withheld from them; and the assembly, therefore, with great submission, lay before Your Majesty herewith, a copy of the said address, with the reply thereto, for Your Majesty's gracious consideration.

"It will by that be seen that the objects contemplated by the assembly are no less than relieving Your Majesty's government permanently from the burthen of the whole civil list of the province, a subject which the assembly humbly conceive to be of great advantage to the parent state, and only requiring that the revenues, from whatever source or sources derived in or collected within the province, should be placed under the control of its legislature."

THE CIVIL LIST

A portion of the Crown-land revenue went to pay what was termed the civil list, which included the salaries of the lieutenant-governor, the judges, the attorney-general, solicitor-general, private secretary, provincial secretary, auditor, receiver-general and commissioner of Crown lands. The latter official received seventeen hundred and fifty pounds sterling per annum besides enormous fees, so that his income was greater than that of the lieutenant-governor. Thomas Baillie, an Irishman, who had been a subaltern in a marching regiment, had filled that office since the year 1824, and continued to [22] hold it until 1851, twenty-seven years in all, when he retired with a pension twice as large as the salary of the present surveyor-general of New Brunswick.

What the Reformers in the legislature of New Brunswick sought to obtain was the control of the public lands, and the disposal of the revenues derived from them. To accomplish this they were willing to undertake to pay the salaries embraced in the civil list, although these salaries were looked upon by the people of the province generally as altogether too large. Yet there were great difficulties in the way of this necessary reform, for King William IV was known to be violently opposed to it. At a later period, 1835, in the course of a conversation with the Earl of Gosford, who had been appointed governor of Lower Canada, "I will never consent," he said with an oath, "to alienate the Crown lands, nor to make the council elective. Mind me, my Lord, the cabinet is not my cabinet. They had better take care, or by − − I will have them impeached."

Such was the language which this king used in regard to his constitutional advisers. It was fortunate for New Brunswick and the other colonies of British North America that at that time he had done his utmost to get rid of his ministers and had been defeated and humiliated, so that they could set him at defiance. But in 1832 they were more disposed to defer to his wishes, and in May of that [23] year we find Lord Goderich, the colonial secretary, writing to Sir Archibald Campbell, the lieutenant-governor of New Brunswick, in the following strain: —

"The preservation to the Crown of the territorial revenue is an object of the first importance, and it would only be resigned on its being clearly proved that the right of the Crown could not be maintained without producing still greater inconvenience. You cannot, therefore, more usefully exert your influence than in endeavouring to prevent the assembly from urging the surrender of this revenue."

CONTROL OF THE REVENUE

The question of the control of the Crown-land or casual and territorial revenues was made the subject of an address to the king by the House of Assembly in 1832. In this it was stated that the expense of collecting these revenues was far greater than it would be under proper management, and it was proposed that they be placed under the control of the legislature, which would undertake the payment of all the necessary expenses of the civil government of the province by making such permanent and other grants as might be necessary for this purpose. The reply to this proposition was received during the legislative session of 1833. In it Lord Goderich, with some appearance of sarcasm, observed that "His Majesty did not consider it necessary at present to call upon the House for a grant of the nature proposed, as he did not anticipate [24] such a falling off in the revenue at his disposal as the House appeared to have apprehended." This reply can hardly be regarded otherwise than as an insult to the House of Assembly, for the meaning of their address to the king was deliberately misrepresented. They were contending for a principle, that the revenue derived from the public domain should be under the control of the legislature, and the amount of the revenue did not enter into the question.

In 1833 the House of Assembly appointed a committee on grievances for the purpose of taking into consideration and investigating all matters in connection with the Crown lands, which were the

subject of complaint. After this committee had reported to the
House, it was resolved to send a deputation to England to endeavour to make some arrangement with the colonial secretary in reference to the Crown lands.

MR. STANLEY'S DESPATCH

The deputies appointed to proceed to England and lay the grievances of the province at the foot of the throne were Charles Simonds
and Edward B. Chandler, both men of wealth, influence and position, and well qualified for the performance of the work with which
they were entrusted. Messrs. Chandler and Simonds arrived in England in June, 1833, and immediately placed themselves in communication with the Right Honourable E. G. Stanley, who was then
colonial secretary. Their report was laid before the legislature in
February, [25] 1834, and the result was highly satisfactory to the
House of Assembly. A few days later a despatch from Mr. Stanley
to Sir Archibald Campbell was laid before the House, in which he
stated the terms on which he should feel that His Majesty might
properly be advised to place the proceeds of the casual and territorial revenue under the control of the assembly of New Brunswick.
He would, he said, be prepared to advise His Majesty to accept a
permanent appropriation by the legislature, duly secured to the
amount of fourteen thousand pounds per annum, and that the
Crown should undertake to charge on any such permanent grant
the salaries of the lieutenant-governor, his private secretary, the
commissioner of Crown lands, provincial secretary, chief-justice,
three puisne judges, the attorney-general, auditor, receiver-general,
the expenses of the indoor establishment of the Crown lands department, and a grant of one thousand pounds to the college. It
would be necessary, Mr. Stanley stated, that any bill passed in consequence of the proposal contained in this despatch should contain
a suspending clause in order that it might be submitted to His Majesty before it was finally assented to. It was also stated, in order to
prevent misunderstanding or delay, that the House should be apprised, that, unless some other fully equivalent and sufficient security could be devised, it would be expected that the Act should provide that the stipulated annual commutation should be payable [26]
out of the first receipts in each year, and that in case of any default
in such payment the whole of the revenue surrendered should re-

vert to the Crown. A committee was appointed to prepare the bill on the subject of the surrender by His Majesty of the casual and territorial revenues of the province. The House of Assembly had previously passed a resolution that the sum of fourteen thousand pounds required by His Majesty's government as a permanent grant for the surrender of the casual and territorial revenues of the province was greater than the charges contemplated to be thereon required, yet that the great desire of the House of Assembly to have this important subject finally settled should induce them to accept the proposal contained in Mr. Stanley's despatch. On the day after this resolution was passed, the lieutenant-governor communicated to the House of Assembly an extract from a despatch received the previous day by him from the Right Honourable Mr. Stanley, dated January 4th, 1834. This extract was as follows: —

"In your message communicating to the assembly the proposal contained in my despatch of the 30th September, you will take care distinctly to explain that the payments expected from the New Brunswick Land Company are not included in the revenue which is offered to the acceptance of the assembly." It is with great regret that an historian of this period must record the receipt of such a [27] despatch from an imperial head of department to a colonial governor, for the spirit displayed in the message was not that of an enlightened statesman, but such as might have been expected from one who was endeavouring to drive the hardest possible bargain with the province of New Brunswick, in order that a number of officials, swollen with pride and enjoying enormous salaries, might not suffer.

NEGOTIATIONS FAIL

A few days after the receipt of this despatch, a resolution was passed by the House in committee, regretting that the additional condition contained in Mr. Stanley's last despatch would prevent the committee recommending to the House further action in the matter of preparing a civil list bill. Thus ended the attempt to settle this vexed question in the year 1834. The House of Assembly, however, still continued to agitate the matter, and to make Sir Archibald Campbell's life a burden to him. On March 7th, they addressed him, asking for accounts in detail of the casual and territorial revenues, and calling for a number of statements which they had not received except in such a shape that they could not be properly understood. They also addressed His Excellency, requesting him to lay before them copies of all official despatches transmitted to him by the secretary of state for the colonies, since he assumed the administration of the government, relating to the subject of the casual and territorial revenues. The reply of His [28] Excellency to the request for more detailed accounts was a courteous one; but while he consented to furnish the accounts requested in detail, it was with the understanding that his compliance was not to be considered as a precedent. He declined, however, to give the names of the parties who had their timber seized or forfeited, or the names of the petitioners for Crown land. He also refused to furnish the accounts of the receiver-general and commissioner of Crown lands, on the ground that they were accounts exclusively between these officers and the Crown.

With regard to the request for his correspondence with the colonial secretary, Sir Archibald Campbell in another message gave a tart refusal, stating that such a request was subversive of the principles and spirit of the British constitution, and that he would ill deserve the confidence put in him by His Majesty were he to hesitate in meeting so dangerous an encroachment, not only on the independence of the executive, but the prerogatives of the British Crown, with a most decided and unqualified refusal. This military officer considered himself a proper exponent of the principles and spirit of the British constitution. He failed to understand that the British constitution rests upon the support of the people, while his system of government was intended to ignore the people altogether.

QUARREL WITH THE GOVERNOR

A few days after the receipt of this message, a [29] resolution was passed by the House of Assembly declaring that the language used by the lieutenant-governor, in his reply to the address of the House, was at variance with all parliamentary precedent and usage, and such as was not called for by the address. Some of the governor's friends attempted to weaken the force of this resolution by an amendment of a milder nature, but their amendment was defeated, and the resolution carried by a vote of fifteen to eight. Another address on the subject of the casual and territorial revenues and civil list was prepared and passed by the assembly for the purpose of being forwarded to His Majesty. It recited the proceedings, in regard to the matter, which had taken place already, and the desire of the House of Assembly to accept the proposition contained in Mr. Stanley's despatch, and expressed the regret of the House at the new condition imposed with regard to the New Brunswick Land Company, which made it impossible to accept the settlement as amended. The House concluded by expressing the hope that the terms proposed in the original despatch might yet be considered definitive, and that the proviso with regard to the New Brunswick Land Company might be withdrawn. This was transmitted to England; but, before the year ended, Sir Archibald Campbell concluded to rid himself of the House of Assembly, which had given him so much annoyance, and accordingly it was dissolved early in November; so that when the legislature [30] met again in January, 1835, the House was a new one, although largely composed of the old members.

[31]

CHAPTER III
WILMOT IN THE LEGISLATURE

Wilmot acquired a good legal practice soon after his admission to the bar, and was recognized as a highly successful advocate in cases before a jury. In the opinion of the legal profession he never was a deeply read lawyer, either as a barrister or as a judge, but in the conduct of a case at *nisi prius* he could hardly have been surpassed. He had the gift which has been possessed by all great advocates, of seizing on the leading feature of a case, and, regardless of all minor issues, pressing it home on the minds of the jury. His eloquent and impressive speeches on behalf of his clients soon began to attract general attention, and the court-house was thronged when it was known that he was about to address a jury. He was speedily marked as the proper person to represent the views of the people in the House of Assembly, and, on a vacancy occurring in the representation of the county of York in consequence of the death of one of the members in the summer of 1834, Wilmot was elected without opposition, none of the government party having the courage to oppose him. Before the time came round for the meeting of the legislature, the House was dissolved by Sir Archibald [32] Campbell, in the hope that he might be able to get an assembly more amenable to his wishes, and, at the general election which followed, Wilmot was again elected, at the head of the poll. At that time he had barely completed his twenty-fifth year. It was a great triumph for Wilmot and the friends of Reform, for all the influence of the friends of the governor and the Family Compact was arrayed against him.

ENTERS THE LEGISLATURE

Mr. Wilmot took his seat as a member of the House of Assembly on January 25th, 1835. Young as he was, he had already made a great reputation as a public speaker, and there was no man in the legislature or in the province who could stand any comparison with him in point of eloquence. Indeed, it is doubtful whether the British North American provinces have ever produced a man who was Wilmot's superior in that style of oratory which is so telling on the hustings or where great masses of men are to be moved. The evidence of this fact does not rest on the testimony of his countrymen alone, for he acquired a wider fame for eloquence than they could give him. At the Portland Railway Convention of 1850, where the ablest men of the Northern States were gathered, he easily eclipsed them all by his brilliant and powerful oratory. The reporters are said to have thrown down their pencils in despair, being unable to keep pace with him as he aroused the enthusiasm of all who heard him by his burning words. Unfortunately, [33] there is no form of ability which is so transient in its effects as this perfervid style of oratory. So much of its potency depends on the action of the speaker, on the glance of his eye and the modulation of his voice, that no report could do justice to it, even if there had been reporters at that time capable of putting down every word he uttered. The speeches of even Gladstone, when reported word for word, read but indifferently when seen in cold type, and no speech of Wilmot's was ever properly reported. He was incapable of writing out a speech after he had delivered it, so that we must take the united testimony of his contemporaries, whether friends or enemies, that he was, upon his own ground, an unequalled speaker.

The House in which he now found himself was not one that was remarkable for its eloquence. Unlike most of the legislatures of the present day, the proportion of lawyers was very small, there being only five in a House of thirty members, and of these five the only one who was an orator was Wilmot. The other twenty-five members were mostly business men and farmers, some of whom could express their views on public questions clearly enough, but had no pretensions to eloquence. Yet it was a good House, and one of its best features was that its members were able to appreciate the worth of the new representative from the county of York.

The aim of Wilmot, when he entered the legislature, [34] was to bring the province into line with the principles of responsible government as understood in the mother country. Yet, looking at the state of New Brunswick then, it is easy to see that the task he had undertaken was one of enormous difficulty. Most of the evils of which the people had been complaining still existed. The casual and territorial revenue was still under the control of the home authorities, the custom-house establishment still remained unreformed, the Family Compact still controlled all the great public offices, and none but members of the Church of England were thought worthy to serve their country in a public capacity.

Two years earlier the executive and legislative councils had been separated; but the change had made little or no improvement in the system of government. The executive council consisted of five members, all of whom held public offices from which they could not be removed by any act of the legislature. The first on the list was Baillie, the surveyor-general, whose record has already been referred to; next came F. P. Robinson, the auditor of the king's casual revenue; another was William F. Odell, whose father had been provincial secretary for twenty-eight years, and who himself filled the same office for thirty-two years. George F. Street, the solicitor-general, was another member of the executive, and the last on the list was John Simcoe Saunders, who was advocate-general and held three or four commissionerships [35] besides. All these men were so solidly entrenched in their positions that it seemed impossible they should ever be disturbed. They formed a solid phalanx opposed to all reform, and they were supported by the governor, Sir Archibald Campbell, most of whose life had been spent in India and who, however well fitted to govern Hindoos, was hardly the man to give laws to white men who claimed to be free.

BECOMES A LEADER

As soon as Wilmot entered the House of Assembly, he began to take a leading part in its debates. The very day he took his seat he was appointed on the committee to prepare an address in reply to the speech from the throne. On the following day he gave notice of a resolution with regard to the boundary between Maine and New Brunswick, a subject that was then coming to the front. A day or two later he brought in a bill to continue the Act to provide for the expenses of judges on circuits. Indeed, no man was more active during that first session than the new member for the county of York.

There were two questions that came up for discussion in which, as a Reformer, he was specially interested,—the salaries of the customs establishment, and the casual and territorial revenue. With regard to the latter, when the House had been sitting about a month, the reply of the colonial secretary to the address of the previous session was laid before it. That address, it will be remembered, [36] related to the offer which had been made to the British government to take over the Crown lands and provide for a civil list of fourteen thousand pounds sterling, the payments expected from the New Brunswick Land Company to be included in this arrangement. The reply of the colonial secretary was as follows: —

"From various parts of the address I infer that the proposal conveyed to the assembly, through my predecessors, must have been misapprehended in more than one important particular; and I have especially remarked the erroneous assumption that, in offering to surrender the proceeds of the Crown lands, it was intended also to give up their management, and to place them under the control of the legislature.

"From the course of their proceedings, as well as the tenor of the present expression of their sentiments, the assembly must be understood to consider it an indispensable condition that the payments of the Land Company should be comprised among the objects to be surrendered to them. This is a condition to which His Majesty's government cannot agree. His Majesty's government would also be unable to recognize the interpretation which was placed on their former offer, so far as regards the control over the lands belonging to the Crown in New Brunswick. Under these circumstances, I can only desire you to convey to the assembly His Majesty's regrets that the objects of [37] their address cannot be complied with, and, adverting to the wide difference between the views entertained by the government and those manifested by the assembly on this subject, it seems to me that no advantage could be anticipated from making any further proposals at present respecting the cession of the territorial revenue."

RENEWED AGITATION

This despatch, which brought a sudden close to the negotiations with regard to the casual and territorial revenues of the province, did not emanate from the government with which the House of Assembly had been previously negotiating, but from a new administration which had just been formed under the premiership of Sir Robert Peel, and which lasted just one hundred and forty-five days. The creation of this administration was due to the action of King

William IV, in dismissing his advisers on the death of Earl Spencer, which removed Lord Althorp from the House of Commons. The king had grown to detest his cabinet for their reforming spirit, but his designs were thwarted by the failure of Sir Robert Peel to form an administration capable of facing the House of Commons. As a consequence, Viscount Melbourne again became premier, and a renewal of the negotiations with the government in regard to the casual and territorial revenues was rendered possible.

The House of Assembly was still determined to keep the question of the casual and territorial revenue [38] to the front, and at a later period in the session another address on this subject was prepared by the House of Assembly, to be laid before His Majesty. In this address the grievances with regard to the management of the Crown lands of New Brunswick were recited, and the willingness of the legislature to provide for the civil establishment of the province was stated. The address urged the benefits that would result to the people of New Brunswick from placing the net proceeds of the Crown-land revenues under the control of the legislature. Attached to this address was a schedule of salaries proposed to be paid out of the casual and territorial revenues, amounting in all to £10,500 currency. The address was transmitted to the governor to be forwarded to His Majesty. No specific answer was ever made to this proposal, a fact which was probably due to the confusion, incident to the change of government, which took place about the time the address reached Downing Street.

CUSTOM-HOUSE SALARIES

Another matter which engaged the attention of the House during this session, and in which Wilmot took an active interest, was the settlement of the salaries of the custom-house officials. Although the surplus revenue from this source went into the provincial treasury, the amount thus received was much less than it ought to have been, in consequence of the large salaries which were paid to the officials. In the year 1830 the amount of custom-house duties collected in the province [39] was £16,616 18s. 11d. sterling, from which was deducted for salaries £7,073 6s., or nearly one-half of the whole amount. The House of Assembly objected to the payment of such large salaries, and in 1831 proposed to the British government to make a permanent annual grant of £4,250 sterling for the payment of customs officials in New Brunswick. This proposal was accepted, and in the following year a bill was passed in accordance with this arrangement. But it was protested against by the customs authorities in England and disallowed because the salaries of the officers of customs were not made the first charge on the revenue. During the session of 1835, an amended bill embracing this provision was passed, and the question was settled for the time. Mr. Wilmot was not satisfied with this arrangement, because it was a violation of the principle that the House of Assembly should have control of the provincial revenue, and he therefore voted against it. Nevertheless, the measure apart from this violation of a fundamental principle, was a gain to the province, as it placed a considerable sum additional in the public treasury.

[41]

CHAPTER IV
WILMOT AS A DELEGATE TO THE COLONIAL OFFICE

Mr. Wilmot took a very active part in the proceedings of the legislature during the session of 1836, and was the moving spirit in the committee of the whole to inquire into the state of the province during that session. The result was the passing by large majorities of a series of twenty-six resolutions condemning the management of the Crown lands office, the composition of the executive council and also of the legislative council, and declaring that the control of the casual and territorial revenues should be placed in the hands of the legislature. These resolutions were made the basis of an address to His Majesty, which was to be carried to England by a deputation of two members of the House of Assembly. This address relates at length the principal facts of the management of the Crown lands and the reasons of the House of Assembly for dissatisfaction therewith. Mr. Wilmot, in recognition of the active part he had taken in this business, was appointed a member of the delegation, the other member being William Crane of Westmorland, a gentleman of experience, wealth and standing in the province. [42] This appointment was the highest compliment that could possibly have been paid to Wilmot's capacity, for the negotiation then to be conducted with the colonial office was of the most important and delicate character, and one which vitally affected the interests of the province.

The colonial secretary at that time was Lord Glenelg, a statesman whose character has been drawn by Sir Henry Taylor, who was then a clerk in the colonial office. "Amiable and excellent as he was," says Taylor, "a more incompetent man could not have been found to fill an office requiring activity and ready judgment. A dart flung at him by Lord Brougham in 1838 points to his notorious defect as a minister called upon to deal with a crisis. The then crisis was that of the Canadian Rebellion." "It is indeed," said Lord Brougham, "a most alarming and frightful state of things, and I am sure must have given my noble friend many a sleepless day." It was probably because of Lord Glenelg's habit of procrastination that the delegates had to remain in London for four months before they were able to bring their business to a conclusion. They arrived there about the middle of June, and it was well on in October before they were able to leave. The result of their work was that an arrangement was made satisfactory both to the British government and to the delegates representing the House of Assembly, by which the casual and territorial revenues were to [43] be transferred to the province, in consideration of the legislature undertaking to provide for a civil list of £14,500 currency annually, for the payment of certain salaries chargeable to that fund. A draft of a Civil List Bill was prepared and agreed to by the lords of the treasury, and the understanding was that this bill should be passed by the legislature, and receive the assent of the lieutenant-governor, when it would immediately become operative.

CIVIL GOVERNMENT BILL

The first clause of this bill transferred the proceeds of the territorial and casual revenues, and of all woods, mines and royalties which had been collected and were then in hand, or which should thereafter be collected, to the provincial treasurer, who was authorized to receive them for the use of the province, while the Act remained in force. The second clause charged the revenues with the payment of £14,500 for a civil list. The third clause enacted that all the surplus over and above the sum of £14,500 currency, should remain in the treasury of the province until appropriated or disposed of by an Act or Acts of the general assembly. The fourth clause gave the lieutenant-governor, with the advice of his executive council, power to expend such sums as they might deem necessary for the prudent management, protection and collection of the said revenues, a detailed account of which was to be laid before the legislature within fourteen days of the commencement of each session, with all [44] vouchers for the same. It was also enacted that all grants or sales of Crown lands should be void, unless the land had been sold at public auction after due notice in the *Royal Gazette*. By this arrangement the House of Assembly had obtained the boon for which it had so long been contending, but there was still one more obstacle to be overcome,—the opposition of the lieutenant-governor, Sir Archibald Campbell, who had entered into a plot with some of the enemies of freedom in the province for the purpose of thwarting, not only the wishes of the House of Assembly, but also the intentions of the home government. As soon as Sir Archibald

Campbell was apprised of the intention of His Majesty's advisers in England to transfer the casual and territorial revenues to the provincial legislature, he commenced a correspondence with the colonial office, pointing out what he deemed to be imperfections in the scheme which they had prepared for the management of the public lands. He pretended to have discovered that there was some error in the calculation of the lords of the treasury with regard to the sum to be paid in lieu of the civil list, and that the amount of £14,500 currency would not be sufficient to defray all the expenditures chargeable on the civil list.

AN OBSTRUCTIVE GOVERNOR

Sir Archibald Campbell, soon after the opening of the session of the legislature, in December 1836, requested the House of Assembly to add a suspending clause to any Civil List Bill they might [45] pass, so that he might forward it to the home government for their approval. As this was entirely contrary to the understanding which had been reached between Messrs. Wilmot and Crane and the colonial secretary, — it being understood that the bill if passed in the form agreed upon would be immediately assented to by the lieutenant-governor, — the House of Assembly very naturally refused to comply with Sir Archibald's wishes. He, however, held firm in his resolution, and the Civil List Bill which had been agreed to by the home authorities, after being passed by both Houses, did not receive his assent. At the close of the session, while the matter was under discussion, at the instigation of the lieutenant-governor one of the executive council, Solicitor-General Street, was sent on a secret mission to Downing Street. The object of this mission was to make such representations to the home authorities as would induce them to delay giving their assent to the Civil List Bill. The truth of the matter seems to have been that Sir Archibald Campbell and his advisers in New Brunswick thought if they could only gain time the Liberal government of England which had granted such favourable terms to the province might be defeated, and a Tory government come into power which would speedily undo all that their predecessors had done, and refuse to grant any concessions to the legislature of New Brunswick. There was great excitement in the province in consequence of the [46] action of the lieutenant-governor, and this excitement was fairly voiced in the House of Assembly, where an address was prepared representing the condition of affairs to His Majesty, and detailing the manner in which the lieutenant-governor had sought to thwart the intentions of the imperial government. This address was passed by a vote of twenty-seven to two, the only members of the House who ventured to stand with the man who occupied Government House being John Ambrose Street and William End.

CIVIL GOVERNMENT BILL PASSED

Messrs. Crane and Wilmot were again appointed a deputation to proceed to England with the address of the House of Assembly, and took their departure two days after it was passed, amidst great popular demonstrations by the citizens of Fredericton. The legislature was prorogued on March 1st, on which day the House of Assembly again requested the lieutenant-governor to pass the Civil List Bill, pointing out that under the arrangements made with the colonial office it was his duty to do so, but their request fell upon deaf ears. In the speech proroguing the legislature, Sir Archibald Campbell stated that he had withheld his assent from this bill because a suspending clause had not been appended to it. These were the last words that this obstinate governor was destined to speak before a New Brunswick legislature. Finding that all his hopes of impeding the progress of the province in the direction of political liberty were in [47] vain, he tendered his resignation to save himself from being removed, as he would have been, for his direct disobedience to the commands of his superiors in England. [1] Sir John Harvey, another soldier, but a man of a very different spirit, was appointed to succeed him as lieutenant-governor. The Civil List Bill was again passed at a special session of the legislature and received the assent of the governor, becoming law on July 17th, 1837. From that time to the present, the province of New Brunswick has controlled the revenues which it derives from its Crown lands and similar sources, and, whether wisely expended or not, the people of this province have at least the satisfaction of knowing that the money is appropriated by their own representatives, and by a government which is responsible to them for its actions.

The death of King William IV took place during the summer of 1837, and brought about another general election. Mr. Wilmot again stood for the county of York and was returned at the head of the poll. This was only a proper recognition of his eminent services to the province in the legislature and as a delegate to England. At this election, Charles Fisher, a young lawyer, was also returned for the county of York. Mr. Fisher, although not so fluent a speaker as Wilmot, was second to no man in the legislature in devotion to Liberal principles, [48] and he proved a most valuable lieutenant in the battle for responsible government which now began. The contest for the control of the Crown lands of the province had been won, but a still more difficult task remained for the friends of constitutional principles to accomplish,—the making of the executive responsible to the people. The members of the House of Assembly had been almost unanimous in demanding the control of the Crown lands, but, when it came to applying the principles of responsible government to the affairs of the province generally, there were many deserters from the ranks of those who had called themselves Reformers. This was partly due to the principles of responsible government not being well understood even by some members of the legislature, and partly to the fact that the question did not touch the self-interest of the members in the same manner as the mismanagement of the Crown lands department had done.

Under a thoroughly constitutional system of government the initiation of money grants would have been in the hands of the executive, but in 1837 not a single member of the executive council had a seat in the House of Assembly. Three of the five members of the executive council were also members of the legislative council, but the two others had no seat in either House, a fact which shows on what lax principles the executive was constructed. The initiation of money grants being in the House of Assembly, any private member [49] had it in his power to move an appropriation of money for any object that he pleased. In this way a system of "log rolling" was inaugurated in the legislature, which resulted in extravagant expenditures and the appropriation of money for objects which, under a better system, would not have received it. It was impossible to put any check upon the expenditure or to keep it within the income under such an arrangement, and one of the first efforts of the Reformers was therefore directed to the removal of this abuse. Unfortunately this was, of all the proposed reforms in the constitution, the one most difficult to carry, and it was not accomplished until after Wilmot had retired from public life.

KING'S COLLEGE

One of the subjects which engaged the attention of Mr. Wilmot, at an early period of his legislative career, was the charter of King's College. This charter had been obtained in 1828 from His Majesty, King George IV, and the legislature had granted the college an endowment of eleven hundred pounds currency a year, in addition to ten hundred pounds sterling granted by the king out of the casual and territorial revenues of the province. The aim of the charter was to make the college a Church of England institution exclusively, for it provided that the bishop of the diocese should be the visitor of the college, and that the president should always be a clergyman in holy orders of the United Church of England and Ireland. No [50] religious test was required of students matriculating or taking degrees in arts, but the council of the college, which was the governing body, was to be composed of members of the Church of England, who, previous to their appointment, had subscribed to the thirty-nine articles. The professors, to the number of seven, who were members of the Church of England, were to be members of the council, so that, although no religious test was required of them, it was reasonably certain that none but persons of that denomination would be appointed to professorships. These terms were much complained of, and surely it was absurd to place a provincial college under the control of a single denomination which could not claim more than one-third of the population of the province as belonging to its communion. It is stated in Fullom's *Life of Sir Howard Douglas*, who was lieutenant-governor of the province at the time, that the charter would have been much less liberal than it was if it had not been for his efforts. The Bishop of Nova Scotia and the Bishop of London desired to confine it entirely to students belonging to the Church of England, and to make subscription to the thirty-nine articles a condition precedent to the granting of degrees in arts. On the other hand, Attorney-General Peters in 1845, when the amendments to the charter were discussed in the legislative council, stated that the charter as originally drafted and sent to England was much [51] more liberal in its provisions than when finally passed, but that in 1828, to the surprise of Sir Howard Douglas, the then existing charter came out copied from one obtained by Dr. Strachan for Upper Canada. If this statement was correct, it affords a singular illustration of the injury that the bigotry of one man can cause to future generations. If King's College had treated all denominations on equal terms, all would have resorted to it for higher education. As it was, it became the college of only a section of the people, the different denominations established colleges of their own, and when finally the connection between the Church of England and King's College was severed and it became the University of New Brunswick, the denominational colleges had become so well established that it could hardly compete with them on equal terms.

AN EXCLUSIVE INSTITUTION

During the session of 1838 Mr. Wilmot, as chairman, submitted to the legislature the report of the select committee which had been appointed to take into consideration the state of the college. In this report it was proposed to make certain alterations in the charter for the purpose of rendering it more acceptable to those who were not in the communion of the Church of England. In 1839 he introduced a bill in the House of Assembly embracing these amendments. The principal changes were to make the lieutenant-governor visitor of the college instead of the bishop, to repeal the section which provided that the president of the college must be [52] a member of the Church of England, and to make persons of every denomination eligible for members of the college council. The professorship of theology was still retained, and students in that course were still required to subscribe to the thirty-nine articles, while services were held in the college morning and evening according to the rites of the Church of England. These changes were certainly of a very moderate character, but they were stoutly resisted by the college authorities and their friends. They put forward the plea that the legislature had no right to alter a royal charter, that to do so was an interference with the royal prerogative, and that the direst consequence would ensue if the constitution of the college was changed. According to their view, a royal charter once granted, the king himself, even with the assistance of both branches of the legislature, could not amend it. The college authorities also denied that they were under the control of the legislature in any way, or responsible to it for their management of the institution, although they were living on money voted by the legislature for its support.

ADDRESS TO THE QUEEN

Wilmot's bill passed the House of Assembly, but was defeated in the legislative council. A similar bill was introduced by him in 1840, but postponed in consequence of a communication from the college council which seemed to show an inclination to yield something to the demands of the public. But a fatal objection to these modifications being [53] accepted was the insistence of the college council that the bishop of the diocese, or in his absence the archdeacon, should be a member of that body. Representatives of the Presbyterians, Methodists and Baptists pointed out in a memorial to the lieutenant-governor that the exclusive character of the council would still remain, as that body would be composed wholly of members of the Church of England. Lord John Russell, the colonial secretary, to whom the matter had been referred, suggested that the college should surrender its charter and that a new one should be prepared embracing the proposed changes, but the college council took no steps to carry these suggestions into effect. This being the case, at Wilmot's instance the House of Assembly proposed an address to the queen setting forth the facts of the case and asking Her Majesty to assent to a bill, a draft of which was enclosed, which the House of Assembly was prepared to pass.

At the session of 1842 Wilmot again introduced the King's College Bill, and it was passed by the House, but again rejected by the legislative council. Early in the session of 1843, the lieutenant-governor communicated to the House by message two despatches from Downing Street on the subject of the college. One of these was from Lord John Russell, and the other from his successor, Lord Stanley. Lord John laid down the doctrine that "it is a principle of undoubted validity that a [54] grant of franchise by the Crown is irrevocable and unalterable by a further exercise of the royal authority unless the power of revocation and change be embodied and reserved in the original grant, or unless the grantees make a voluntary surrender of their franchises." Lord John had evidently forgotten his English history, or he would have known that English kings on many occasions had revoked charters granted by themselves or their predecessors. [2] Lord John desired the college to surrender its charter and accept a new one, but Lord Stanley and the law officers of the Crown whom he had consulted held a different view, and thought that a new charter could be granted to supersede the old. Both colonial secretaries were desirous that the changes in the constitution of the college should be effected by a new royal charter. But this did not suit the views of the House of Assembly, and after another college bill had been defeated in the House and rejected by the council, on March 20th, 1843, the following resolution, which was moved by Mr. Wilmot, was passed by the House without a division: —

"Whereas, The assembly, during several years past, have endeavoured, without success, to effect certain reasonable modifications in the charter of King's College; and whereas those modifications as contained in the bill which has been rejected by [55] the legislative council, during the present session, have been loudly and repeatedly called for by numerous petitions from nearly every county in the province, while no petition has ever been presented against those modifications; and whereas it is in vain to expect the amount of public benefit from the institution which its munificent endowment from the provincial revenue should ensure; therefore,

"*Resolved*, That this House have learned with much regret and disappointment that a majority of the legislative council have rejected the said bill during the present session; and further

"*Resolved*, That this House should persevere in their endeavours to amend the said charter by legislative enactment, and not resort to an address to the throne for a new charter; and that this House will steadfastly adhere to the principle that all the educational establishments of the province, which are endowed from the colonial revenues, whether incorporated by royal charter or otherwise, should be at all times subject to the supervision of the local legislature."

COLLEGE CHARTER AMENDED

This resolution embodied a great principle to which the House of Assembly was determined to adhere, and which was very soon carried out. In 1844 the college amendment bill was again rejected by the council, but this was the last effort of that reactionary body to defeat the wishes of the people. At the session of 1845, the college bill was again [56] introduced by Mr. Wilmot, and this time it passed both Houses. But like many important bills of that day it was reserved for Her Majesty's pleasure and although passed in March, 1845, it was not until December, 1846, that it received the royal assent and became law.

FOOTNOTES:

[1] This is shown by the correspondence of Sir John Harvey with the colonial office. Sir John was then governor of Prince Edward Island.

[2] Charles II annulled the charter of Massachusetts, and disposed in a similar fashion of the charter of the city of London, as well as of many English towns.

[57]

CHAPTER V
LORD JOHN RUSSELL ON TENURE OF OFFICE

In the session of 1840 Sir John Harvey, the lieutenant-governor, communicated to the legislature a despatch which he had received from Lord John Russell a short time before. This dealt with the question of the tenure of public offices in the gift of the Crown throughout the British colonies. Lord John had been struck by the fact that, while the governor of a colony was liable to have his commission revoked at any time, the commissions of all other public officials were very rarely recalled except for positive misconduct. In New Brunswick offices had been held generally for life and sometimes for two lives, as was the case with the Odells, father and son, who filled the position of secretary of the province for sixty years. One attorney-general of the province had held office for twenty-four years, another for nineteen years and a third for twenty years. One surveyor-general held office for thirty-three years and another for almost thirty years. Under such a system, it was clear that responsible government could make no advance, for these officials held their positions quite independently of the wishes of the legislature. Lord John Russell thought that the time had [58] come when a different course should be followed, and his despatch was for the purpose of announcing to the lieutenant-governor the rules which would hereafter be observed in the province of New Brunswick. He said:—

"You will understand, and cause it to be made generally known, that hereafter the tenure of colonial offices held during Her Majesty's pleasure will not be regarded as equivalent to a tenure during good behaviour, but that not only such officers will be called upon to retire from the public service as often as any sufficient motives of public policy may suggest the expediency of that measure, but that a change in the person of the governor will be considered as a sufficient reason for any alterations which his successor may deem it expedient to make in the list of public functionaries, subject, of course, to the future confirmation of the sovereign.

"These remarks do not extend to judicial offices, nor are they meant to apply to places which are altogether ministerial, and which do not devolve upon the holders of them duties, in the right discharge of which the character or policy of the government are directly involved. They are intended to apply rather to the heads of departments than to persons serving as clerks, or in similar capacities under them. Neither do they extend to officers in the services of the lords commissioners of the treasury. The functionaries who will be chiefly, though not exclusively, affected by them, are the colonial [59] secretary, the treasurer or receiver-general, the surveyor-general, the attorney-general and solicitor-general, the sheriff or provost marshal, and other officers, who under different designations from these, are entrusted with the same or similar duties. To this list must be also added the members of the council, especially in those colonies in which the legislative and executive councils are distinct bodies.

"The application of these rules to officers to be hereafter appointed will be attended with no practical difficulty. It may not be equally easy to enforce them in the case of existing officers, and especially of those who may have left this country for the express purpose of accepting the offices they at present fill. Every reasonable indulgence must be shown for the expectations which such persons have been encouraged to form. But even in these instances it will be necessary that the right of enforcing these regulations should be distinctly maintained, in practice as well as in theory, as often as the public good may clearly demand the enforcement of them. It may not be unadvisable to compensate any such officers for their disappointment, even by pecuniary grants, when it may appear unjust to dispense with their services without such an indemnity."

AN HISTORIC DESPATCH

This despatch produced consternation among those who had been accustomed to regard their offices as held on a life tenure, but it was looked upon [60] by all the friends of good government as the beginning of a new and better order of things with respect to the public services. The matter was considered by a committee of the whole House a few days after the despatch was received, and an effort was made by Wilmot to have a favourable vote with regard to it. But although the friends of the old Family Compact always professed to be extremely loyal and to pay great deference to the wishes of the British government, on this occasion they pursued a different course. A majority of the House voted down a resolution which affirmed that this despatch should be "highly satisfactory," "affording, as it does, the most satisfactory proof of a sincere desire on the part of our Most Gracious Queen and her government to infuse principles in the administration of colonial affairs strictly analogous to the principles of the British constitution." Instead of passing this sensible resolution the committee, by the casting vote of the chairman, passed the following absurd amendment: —

"*Resolved*, As the opinion of this committee, that there is nothing in the despatch of the Right Honourable Lord John Russell, now under consideration, to call forth any expression from the House on the subject of colonial government, and that in the event of any occurrence taking place to disturb the present happy political state of the province, the House cannot but entertain the opinion that any loyal and dutiful representations which [61] they may have occasion to lay at the foot of the throne will receive, as they have always done, the royal consideration."

The vote on the original resolution was fifteen to thirteen, so that, although defeated, it had a strong support in the House, yet it was years before the principles embodied in the despatch of Lord John Russell were carried into full effect in New Brunswick.

OFFICIAL SALARIES

When the Civil List Bill was passed in 1837, the salaries of the public officials which were provided for in it were placed on a very liberal scale. The lieutenant-governor was to receive £3,500 sterling, or almost double the present salary of the lieutenant-governor of New Brunswick. The commissioner of Crown lands was to have £1,750 sterling, or about five times as much as the present holder of that office; the provincial secretary got £1,430 sterling, or more than three times as much as the secretary of the province now receives. All the other salaries were in the same proportion, and on a scale altogether beyond the means of the province. It was admitted by Lord Glenelg, when the arrangements were being made for the transfer of the casual and territorial revenues, that these salaries might require modification, and he suggested that the legislative council and the House of Assembly should at some future day present him with their views on this subject. At the session of 1837, a committee of the House of Assembly, of which Wilmot was a member, [62] reported in favour of a reduced scale of salaries, and this report was adopted by the House. During the same year, a committee of the council recommended that the salary of the surveyor-general or commissioner of Crown lands should be reduced to twelve hundred pounds currency. This reduction was protested against by Mr. Baillie, who had held the office for many years, but it was thought to be reasonable by Lord Glenelg. The executive council, however, took no steps to effect this reduction, possibly because Mr. Baillie himself was a member of that body. At the instance of Mr. Wilmot, the matter was taken up by the House at the session of 1839, and a strongly worded resolution passed censuring the executive council for not carrying into effect the reduction of the salary of the surveyor-general, according to the views of Lord Glenelg. At a later period in the same session, a committee, of which Wilmot was an active member, laid before the House a scale of salaries which they had prepared and which they considered sufficient for the public officials embraced in the civil list. Under this scale, the salary of the surveyor-general was reduced to £600 currency, and that of the provincial secretary to the same amount. This report was not accepted by the House. There were strong interests working for the retention of the existing salaries, and it was not until a much later period that the salaries of the public officials were placed on a footing [63] that agreed in some measure with the means of the province.

At the session of 1842, Wilmot was an active member of a committee which was appointed to take into consideration the subject of fees and emoluments of the public officers, and at a later period in the session they made a report recommending that all fees should go into the treasury of the province and that all public officers should receive a certain fixed salary. They presented with their report a scale of salaries which they considered sufficient, which gave the provincial secretary, surveyor-general and attorney-general each six hundred pounds. Bills were introduced for the purpose of carrying these recommendations into effect, but, although passed by the House, they were rejected by the council, which for many years was the graveyard of all measures for the improvement of the province.

RESPONSIBLE GOVERNMENT

The general election of 1842 was mainly fought on the Reform issue, and the question of responsible government was discussed on every hustings. Unfortunately very few of the candidates who offered their services as legislators had a clear idea of what responsible government really meant, and some of the gentlemen who were not ashamed to confess their ignorance of the principles of the British constitution were men of education and position, from whom better things might have been expected. Mr. Robert L. Hazen, an eminent lawyer, who was [64] a candidate for the representation of the city of St. John, declared in his nomination speech that he never met with any one who could explain to him satisfactorily what responsible government meant. Mr. Humbert, one of the candidates for St. John County, was entirely averse to the new principles. "And what," he asked, "are these principles?" "Why," he would ask, "should the old system be altered; it had never given cause for complaint, it had always worked well,—then why should the people complain?" He was not in favour of any innovations on British colonial government. Very few people understood what responsible government meant. He hardly understood it himself. It was, in his opinion, just introducing another branch into our government. He was not in favour of the government initiating the money votes. He was always sensitive about the rights of the House—to them ought the power of originating the supplies to belong, and to none other— and if returned he would oppose the measure.

Such absurdities as the above would not be worth quoting, but for the light they throw on the views of the average New Brunswick politician of that period. Mr. Humbert had been for many years a member of the House of Assembly, and yet he had been unable to understand the significance of the changes which the Reformers proposed in the constitution of the country. The result of the election in St. John showed that the people of [65] that city and county were quite indifferent to the new doctrines. For the county, Mr. Partelow was at the head of the poll, and that gentleman on the hustings had declared that he was opposed to any change in the constitution. He went into the House, he said, under a constitution of fifty years' standing, and he was determined to leave it as he found it, unimpaired. He disapproved of the initiation of money votes being placed in the hands of the executive. He thought "such a system would be wrong and pernicious in the extreme."

REFORMERS DEFEATED

When the legislature met in January 1843, it was found that the Reformers were in the minority. Mr. Partelow was determined to make this fact very clear, for in nominating the speaker he made a speech of some length in which he declared that the time had come for testing the principles on which the House should act, and with this object in view he would throw down the gauntlet to the friends of responsible government by nominating Mr. J. W. Weldon, to fill the chair. This gentleman was a very fit representative of the old system, for besides being a member for Kent, he filled almost all the offices in that county which one man could hold. He was postmaster of Richibucto, deputy treasurer for the port of Richibucto, issuer of marriage licenses for the county of Kent, keeper of the seals and clerk of the peace and of the inferior court of common pleas, and registrar of probates for the same county. [66]

Mr. Wilmot was nominated for the speakership by Mr. Hill, of Charlotte, but declined to run; the odds were too great, and so Mr. Weldon, the opponent of responsible government, was elected without opposition. This was an unsatisfactory result after so many years of conflict, but the friends of Reform, although they had to admit defeat, were neither daunted nor discouraged. They knew that many other questions besides the abstract one of the adoption of responsible government had influenced the recent election, and that the new principles had been blamed for results that would have been avoided if they had been in operation. For instance, the transfer of the casual and territorial revenues to the treasury of the province in 1837 had placed a very large sum, amounting to £150,000, at the disposal of the legislature. All this money had been dissipated by extravagant grants, and in 1842 the province was actually in debt. Many ignorant electors were made to believe that this result was due to the Reformers who had been the means of obtaining this money, which the legislature had squandered; and this feeling was so strong in the county of York, that Messrs. Wilmot and Fisher stood lower on the poll than the two anti-Reformers who were elected with them.

[67]

CHAPTER VI
THE READE APPOINTMENT

Although elected in opposition to responsible government, the legislature of 1843 at its first session took one important step in favour of Reform. The arrangement by which the executive and legislative councils were separated, which had come into force ten years before, although a decided improvement on the old state of affairs, did not produce universal satisfaction. [3] The constitution of the legislative council was complained of, and it was described as an obstructive body which disregarded the wishes of the people. Bills of the utmost importance, which had been passed by large majorities in the House of Assembly, and which were demanded by the people, were frequently rejected by the council without being even discussed. Most of its members were opposed to any change in the constitution of the province, and everything which seemed to be in the direction of giving power to the people was denounced as an innovation and condemned as an infringement of [68] the vested rights of the council. One of the chief causes of complaint against the council was their rejection of every bill for the amendment of the charter of King's College. Wilmot had so frequently had his efforts in this direction nullified by the council that he introduced a resolution in the assembly condemning the conduct of that body for rejecting the college bill, and the council retaliated by unanimously voting this a breach of privilege. [4] The complaints of the House of Assembly against the legislative council were now embodied in an address to the queen. In this address it was stated that in the opinion of the House the legislative council should be composed of persons not only representing all the leading interests of the province, but so independent in respect to property and so free from official control as to form a constitutional check on the executive. Although, by the laws that existed then, members of the assembly were required to be possessed of real estate to the value of two hundred pounds, over and above all encumbrances, there was no property qualification whatever required for members of the legislative council. The address of the House expressed the opinion that members of the council should be required to possess a certain amount of real estate, and that their seats should be vacant on the loss of this

qualification, or on their becoming bankrupt, [69] or public default-
ers, or from neglect to give their attendance for a given time without
leave of the lieutenant-governor. The address also stated that the
constitution of the legislative council was defective and objectionable in other respects, because, of the eighteen members who composed it, a great proportion held offices at the pleasure of the
Crown, and the principal officers of the government usually formed
a majority of the members present. It was also complained that
members of the Church of England had too great a preponderance
in the council, the only members not of that communion being one
Presbyterian and one Baptist.

THE LEGISLATIVE COUNCIL

At the next session of the legislature, despatches from Lord Stanley were laid before the House of Assembly in which it was stated
that the council would be increased in number to twenty-one, and
four new members of the council were to be appointed. The new
members then appointed were T. H. Peters, Admiral Owen, William
Crane and George Minchin, while the Hon. Thomas Baillie, the
surveyor-general, the Hon. Mr. Lee, the receiver-general, the Hon.
James Allanshaw, of St. Andrews, and the Hon. Harry Peters, of
Gagetown, retired. No doubt the retirement of two officials who
received large salaries was some improvement, but the council required further remodelling before it could be said to be an efficient
body, or one in sympathy with the inhabitants of the province. [70]

The legislative council has now ceased to exist, and it may be said
of it that it was never a very satisfactory body for legislative purposes. Perhaps the original composition of it created such a prejudice against legislative councils as to hamper its activities; and, from
having been at first merely the echo of the wishes of the governor, it
became latterly, to a large extent, the echo of the wishes of the government. Gradually it became relieved of its official members, and
in its last years no head of a department ever occupied a seat in the
legislative council; for it was thought, and rightly, that the power
ought to be in the House, where the responsibility to the people was
most felt, and that it was not wise to place an official whose department expended large sums of money in a body which properly
had no control over the public expenditure. The legislative council

had undoubtedly from time to time many able and useful members, and, at certain periods in the history of the province, particularly during the confederation discussions, it took a firm stand in favour of measures which seemed essential to the prosperity of the British North American provinces. No one can deny that at that time it exercised an authority fully equal to that of the Lower House, but it cannot be doubted that some of this work was done at the expense of the proper balance of the constitution. Such an exercise of unusual authority on the part of a body not elected by the people may serve a purpose at a [71] particular crisis, but cannot be commended as an example, and if frequently repeated would end in the destruction of the constitution.

THE COUNCIL'S RECORD

The legislative council lost a considerable proportion of its able men at the time of confederation by the removal of eleven of its members to the senate of Canada, although one or two remained with it who were not inferior to any of those who then took their departure. The new members who came in as their successors were naturally inferior to the old in practical experience and ability, and this had, no doubt, an influence on the future of the House. The example of Ontario, which was able to conduct its affairs with one House, showed that two independent branches of the legislature were by no means necessary, and that the council might be abolished with safety. No doubt it was difficult to bring this about among a people who had been trained to believe that there was something essential to legislation in the balance of king, lords, and commons, making up one legislative body. But in the course of time the electors began to think that the council was not exactly the proper equivalent of the House of Lords, and the lieutenant-governor very far from standing in the position of a king. Old prejudices in favour of a constitution framed after a particular model are difficult to remove, but, in the case of New Brunswick, these prejudices were at length overcome, and it is safe to say that in the course of time all the provincial legislatures [72] of Canada will consist of but a single chamber. It is equally safe to assert that under the new system the work of legislation will be as well done as it was under the old.

The session of the legislature in 1843 came to an end on April 11th, and on the seventeenth of the same month Wilmot became a member of the government. His appointment had been preceded by the resignation of five members of the government—Messrs. Black, Shore, Robinson, Odell and Crane—and by the appointment of Messrs. E. B. Chandler, Hugh Johnston, John Montgomery and Robert L. Hazen, to fill the vacancies thus created. Of the retiring members two—Messrs. Black and Shore—were members of the legislative council; one of them, Mr. Crane, was a member of the House of Assembly, while the other two were officials who did not belong to either branch of the legislature. Of the new members of the executive council, Messrs. Chandler and Johnston were members of the legislative council, Messrs. Hazen and Wilmot were members of the House of Assembly, while Mr. Montgomery had no seat in either House. The executive council as made up at that time included four members of the legislative council, three members of the House of Assembly and Mr. Montgomery, who did not become a member of the House of Assembly until three years later. There is no doubt that the composition of the new executive council was more in accordance with correct [73] principles than its predecessor; yet little could be expected from it in the way of Reform, for Wilmot was the only member who was in favour of responsible government.

ENTERS THE GOVERNMENT

Mr. Wilmot has been censured for entering a government composed of men who were opposed to the liberal views he held on public questions. It was thought by many that his conduct in this respect looked too much like a surrender of his principles for the sake of office or official position, and it certainly would have been better if he had continued in Opposition. Yet we can easily conceive that he may have thought at the time he could do more for the cause of Reform inside the government than out of it, and, although this proved to be an error, it was a natural one for which it is not difficult to find an excuse. Fortunately for the cause of Reform, Wilmot's connection with the government did not last long at that time. A storm was gathering in an unexpected quarter which was destined to wreck the government, and to cause some of its Conservative members to reconsider their opinions with reference to some questions which until then they had regarded as fixed and unchangeable.

It has been already stated that the governor of the province made such appointments to office as he pleased, usually without the advice of his council. He was supposed to have the power to do this as the representative of the sovereign and in the [74] exercise of what was termed "the royal prerogative." In this way persons were frequently appointed to offices who were not residents of the province, and in all other cases appointments were given to the members of certain favoured families. In 1834, a vacancy was created on the supreme court bench by the death of Chief-Justice Saunders. Ward Chipman was appointed chief-justice in place of Mr. Saunders, and the vacant puisne judgeship was given to James Carter, who afterwards became chief-justice of the province. Carter was a young Englishman then living in London, and was certainly no better qualified to fill the position of judge than many natives of the province, so that it was regarded as a gross insult to the members of the New Brunswick bar, to give such an appointment to a stranger. Yet so slow was public opinion to make itself felt in regard to the evil of the appointing power being given to the governor without qualification, that ten years later the House of Assembly presented an address to Sir Charles Metcalfe, governor-general of Canada, expressing the high sense entertained by them, as representatives of the people of New Brunswick, of the "constitutional stand" taken by him in maintaining the prerogative of the Crown in the then recent memorable "conflict." [5] The city of St. John [75] also, to show its loyalty, presented a similar address; and one signed by one thousand persons was sent from the county of York.

SIR CHARLES METCALFE

Yet nothing can be more clear than that the stand taken by Sir Charles Metcalfe in 1844 was wholly wrong, for it consisted in refusing to consult with his council in regard to appointments, and in making appointments contrary to their advice. What would the people of Canada say to-day to a governor-general who insisted on appointing men to office against the advice of his cabinet? Yet it was for doing this that the New Brunswick House of Assembly, the city and county of St. John and the county of York actually grovelled in the dust before this despotic governor, thus approving of all his acts. Such abasement and subserviency to an unconstitutional governor was certain to bring its own punishment, and it came much sooner than any one could have anticipated. On Christmas Day of the same year the Hon. William Franklin Odell, who had been provincial secretary for thirty-two years, died at Fredericton. Mr. Odell's father had [76] been secretary before him from the foundation of the province, so that the Odell family had held that important and highly lucrative office for sixty years.

The governor at this time was Sir William Colebrooke, and on January 1st, 1845, just one week after the death of Mr. Odell, he appointed his son-in-law, Alfred Reade, who was a native of England and a stranger to the province, to the vacant office. The gentlemen who had been most prominent in shouting their approval of the "constitutional stand" taken by Sir Charles Metcalfe, now suddenly discovered that Sir William Colebrooke's conduct in making this appointment without consulting his council, was a fearful outrage, and their distress was pitiable to behold. Several members of the government, including such zealous upholders of the prerogative as the Hon. Robert L. Hazen, of St. John, at once resigned their positions. A communication from three of them — Hugh Johnston, E. B. Chandler and R. L. Hazen — addressed to His Excellency gave as their reasons for resigning that they could not justify the exercise of the prerogative of the Crown in respect to Mr. Reade's appointment, because they felt that "the elevation to the highest offices of trust and emolument of individuals whose character, services, and claims to preferment, however appreciated elsewhere, are entirely unknown to the country generally, is prejudicial to the best interests [77] of the province." They did not, however, make it a ground of objection that the appointment of Mr. Reade was forwarded for the royal approbation without the advice or concurrence of the council. These gentlemen evidently thought it was too early for them to eat the words in regard to the prerogative of the Crown, of which they had been so free a few months before, but they showed their true characters by deserting the governor because he had been foolish enough to believe that their profuse expressions in favour of the royal prerogative were sincere.

RESIGNATION

Mr. Wilmot, who also resigned, sent a separate communication to the lieutenant-governor in which he stated what he considered to be the true constitutional doctrine which should govern such matters. He said:—

"In the first place, I consider it justly due to the people of this province, that all the offices of honour and emolument in the gift of the administration of the government should be bestowed upon inhabitants of the province who have made this country their home, and, in the cases of the principal offices, those persons should be preferred who have claims for public services rendered to the province, and who can command the respect and confidence of the country. With these views, which I hope I shall ever retain, I must necessarily disapprove of the appointment in question, as I can only look upon Mr. Reade as a comparative [78] stranger and a transient person, while, at the same time, I am of opinion that he has no claim whatever on the ground of public services rendered to this province.

"It would be in vain for the parents of our youth to make every exertion in order to qualify their sons for the higher offices of the province, if the avenues to honourable and profitable preferment are to be thus closed against them; and I therefore cannot but view the appointment under consideration as an act of great injustice to the people of this country; and I can safely assure Your Excellency that it will be thus considered throughout the length and breadth of the province.

"Your Excellency is well aware that ever since I have had the honour of having a seat in the council, I have approved of, and advocated those principles of colonial government which are now in full operation in Canada, which have been distinctly enunciated by the present government in the House of Commons, and which require the administration to be conducted by heads of departments responsible to the legislature, and holding their offices contingently upon the approbation and confidence of the country as expressed through the representatives of the people. Still entertaining a strong attachment to those principles from a clear constitutionality, and, from a conscientious belief in their safe and practical adaptation to a British colony enjoying the privileges of a representative [79] form of government, I can see no sufficient reason for withholding their salutary influence from the loyal and intelligent people of this province; and considering it more advisable that a gradual advancement should be made by the government itself towards those principles as opportunities may offer, than that a concession in gross should hereafter be made to the urgent demands of the country, I am of the opinion that the provincial secretary should now be brought into the executive government, and should hold a seat in one of the Houses of the legislature—his tenure of office being contingent upon the successful administration of the government; and therefore, as the appointment in question has been made irrespective of any of these conditions, I am bound to give it my opposition."

REMONSTRANCE OF THE ASSEMBLY

When the House met in the latter part of January, the Reade appointment immediately became the subject of discussion, and by the vote of twenty-four to six, an address was passed to Her Majesty the Queen, condemning the appointment, not, as the members said, because they questioned "in the remotest degree the prerogative in its undoubted right to make such appointments," but because they thought that the right of appointment had been improperly or unjustly exercised. In other words, the members of the House of Assembly surrendered the principle that appointments should be made by the governor, with the advice of his [80] executive, and only objected to the Reade appointment because, in their opinion, some one else should have been chosen. It is easy to see that in subscribing to this address the members of the House stultified themselves; for if it was a part of the prerogative of the Crown to make appointments without the advice of the council, surely the exercise of the prerogative in the appointment of a particular individual could not be fairly questioned. The result of the difficulty, however, was the cancelling of Mr. Reade's appointment by the home government. This decision was communicated to the House of Assembly by message on February 3rd, 1846. The despatch from the colonial office, upon which the lieutenant-governor acted, was written on March 31st, 1845, and must have been received by him at Fredericton not later than the last of April. But notwithstanding this despatch Mr. Reade held office until July 17th, so it will be seen that Sir William Colebrooke was in no hurry to carry out the wishes of the home government. Lord Stanley, the writer of the despatch in question, expressed the opinion that public employment should be bestowed on the natives or settled inhabitants of the province, and he thought that Mr. Reade did not come under this description. He closed his despatch with the following singular statement: —

READE'S APPOINTMENT CANCELLED

"I observe with satisfaction that the House of Assembly have not only abstained from complicating [81] the subject with any abstract question of government, but have rejected every proposal for laying down formal principles upon such questions. The House has, I think, in this course done justice to the earnest desire of Her Majesty that the colonial administration generally should be conducted in harmony with the wishes of her people, whatever may be the variations arising out of local considerations and the state of society in various colonies, subject to which that principle may be carried into practice; and it is anxiously hoped that the same wise forbearance which has led the House of Assembly to decline the unnecessary discussion of subjects of so much delicacy, may lead them also to regard the practical decision now announced as the final close of the controversy, and to unite in the promotion, not of objects of party strife and rivalry, but of the more substantial and enduring interests of the colony which they represent." If these words have any meaning, they seem to show that at that date the British government believed the right of appointment to be in the Crown, without reference to the council, and that they were unwilling that any general principle should be laid down by the legislature of the province which conflicted with this view.

FOOTNOTES:

[3] This change had been effected by a royal commission under the signet and sign-manual dated December 3d, 1832. There is nothing in the records of the province to show why this was done. Neither the council nor the House of Assembly had asked for it. The Nova Scotia council was not divided until 1838.

[4] Mr. Wilmot's resolution was carried in the assembly without a division, so that he had the solid support of the popular branch of

the legislature, yet little good was to be expected from such votes in the House.

[5] The resolution to present this address was strongly opposed by Mr. Wilmot and his colleague, Mr. Fisher, who both declared the conduct of Lord Metcalfe to be contrary to the principles of responsible government. Mr. Wilmot's speech led to a singular result. He was attacked in the *Loyalist* newspaper for his opposition to the address, and this attack having been brought to the notice of the House of Assembly was voted a breach of privilege. Messrs. Doak and Hill, the proprietors of the paper, were arrested on the warrant of the speaker and committed to prison. On the application of their counsel, Mr. D. S. Kerr, they were released by Mr. Justice Carter on a writ of *habeas corpus*. Doak and Hill both brought actions against the speaker, Mr. Weldon, and the result was a decision of the Supreme Court of New Brunswick that the House of Assembly had not the power to arrest and imprison the publisher of a libel on a member of the House touching his conduct and proceedings in the House.

[83]

CHAPTER VII
WILMOT'S VIEWS ON EDUCATION

Among the questions in which Wilmot took a deep interest was that of education. His views on this subject were far in advance of those of most of his contemporaries. Education was in a very unsatisfactory condition in the province of New Brunswick when he entered public life, and it continued in that condition for many years afterward. If we may judge from the statute-book, the founders of the province had very little appreciation of the advantages of education, for no law was passed with a view to the establishment of public schools until the year 1805. In that year "An Act for encouraging and extending literature in this province" was passed, under the provisions of which a public grammar school was established in the city of St. John, which received a grant of one hundred pounds for the purpose of assisting the trustees to procure a suitable building for school uses, and also an annual grant of one hundred pounds for the support of the master. The same Act provided for the establishment of county schools, and the sections relating to them, being limited in respect to time, were continued by 50th George III, Chap. 33 to the year 1816, when they expired and were [84] replaced by "An Act for the establishment of schools in the province." This Act expired in 1823, and in its place "An Act for the encouragement of parish schools" was passed the same year. This last Act was repealed by "An Act in relation to parish schools" passed in 1833, which continued in force for many years. All these Acts were essentially the same in principle, as they provided for government aid to teachers who had been employed to teach schools in the parishes under the authority of the school trustees. The Act of 1833, which was considered to be a great improvement on former Acts, provided for the appointment of three school trustees in each parish by the sessions, and these trustees were charged with the duty of dividing the parishes into districts and directing the discipline of the schools. They were required to certify once a year to the lieutenant-governor as to the number of schools in their parish, the number of scholars and other particulars, and on their certificate the teacher drew the government money. This money was granted at the rate of twenty pounds for a male teacher who had taught school a year, or ten pounds for six months, and ten pounds for a female teacher who had taught school a year, or five pounds for six months, provided the inhabitants of the school district had subscribed an equal amount for the support of the teacher, or supplied board, washing and lodging to the teacher in lieu of the money. Thus a male teacher in [85] a district where a school was always kept, would receive for his year's work his board, lodging and washing, and twenty pounds in money; and a female teacher ten pounds. Such a rate of remuneration was not well calculated to attract competent persons, and the result was very unsatisfactory. Most of the teachers employed were old men who had a mere smattering of learning and who were very incompetent instructors. They usually lodged with the parents of the pupils, living at each house in proportion to the number of scholars sent. This system, which raised them but one degree above the condition of paupers, was not conducive to their comfort or self-respect. As there was no uniformity in the books prescribed and no sufficient educational test, the results of such teaching were not likely to be satisfactory. Sometimes the teacher was a woman who eked out a scanty subsistence by communicating her small learning to a few scholars whom she gathered in her kitchen. Generally, however, the school building was a log hut without any of those appliances which are now regarded as essential to the proper instruction of youth.

PROVINCIAL GRAMMAR SCHOOLS

In 1816 an Act was passed providing for the establishment of grammar schools in the several counties of the province. At that period St. John and St. Andrews had already grammar schools which had been established under separate Acts, and Fredericton had an academy or college, which was [86] founded by a provincial charter granted by Lieutenant-Governor Carleton in 1800. The counties of St. John, Charlotte and York were therefore excepted from the operation of the general Act for the establishment of grammar schools. This Act, after being amended in 1823, was finally repealed by the Act of 1829, which endowed King's College at Fredericton and made new provisions for the establishment and support of grammar schools throughout the province. King's College at a later period developed into the University of New Brunswick. It had its beginning in the original charter of 1800, already referred to, which established the College of New Brunswick. In the same year the governor and trustees of the College of New Brunswick received a grant, under the great seal of the province, of a considerable tract of land in and near Fredericton for the support of that institution of learning. Until the year 1829, the New Brunswick College was merely a classical school receiving from the legislature annually two hundred and fifty pounds, which was the same amount then allowed to the St. John Grammar School.

MADRAS SCHOOLS

At an early period, the attention of the people of that province was directed to what was called the Madras system of national schools as conducted by Dr. Bell, the real founder of the system being Joseph Lancaster. This system depends for its success on the use of monitors, who are selected from among the senior pupils to instruct the younger [87] ones. It was supposed at the time to be a notable discovery, but, like other short cuts to learning, has fallen out of favour. In July, 1818, the first Madras school was established in St. John by a Mr. West from Halifax. This was a boys' school; and a school for girls, on the same system, was opened a year or two later. In 1819, a Madras school charter was procured under the great seal of the province, and the Madras school system established on a substantial foundation. The province gave a grant of two hundred and fifty pounds for the erection of a suitable building in St. John, and the National Society in England contributed to its support. This charter was confirmed by an Act passed in 1820. The St. John school was to be regarded as the central school, but it was the design of the charter that the benefits of the system should be extended to other parts of the province, and this was accordingly done. The Madras schools received liberal appropriations of money, and large grants of land, and they continued to exist until the introduction of the free school system in 1872. Two or three of them, indeed, continued in operation after that time, but they had lost their original character and had become simply Church of England schools, that denomination having appropriated the Madras school endowments to the support of schools in which its principles and creed were taught. In 1900, by Act of the legislature, the Madras school property was handed over to the diocesan synod of [88] Fredericton, with the exception of about ten thousand dollars, which went to the University of New Brunswick.

From the day when Wilmot became a member of the House of Assembly in 1835, he began to press upon the attention of that body the necessity for an improvement in the schools of the province. But the same spirit of apathy which prevailed with regard to purely political questions affected the legislature with respect to education. The people throughout the province were not prepared to make the sacrifices necessary to obtain sufficient schools. Their attitude with regard to education was well described in a speech made by Wilmot in 1846, when Mr. Brown, of Charlotte, brought in his bill to provide for a normal or proper training school for the education of those who were to become teachers. This bill did not become law, in consequence of the opposition raised against it in the legislature on the ground of expense. It was estimated that it would cost an additional two thousand pounds to provide a normal school, and this sum the men who were at the head of the government were not willing to pay for the purpose of giving the children of the province properly trained teachers. Wilmot's speech on that occasion concluded as follows: —

PARISH SCHOOLS

"Before I sit down I must again revert to the greatest difficulty which has to be encountered to render the provisions of that bill effective in promoting [89] a better system of education in the parish schools. This is a difficulty which in this country legislation cannot reach — I earnestly wish it could. I mean the apathy of the parents themselves. The honourable member now in the chair can bear me witness as to the extent to which this apathy prevails in this county at this day. That honourable member, when out of the chair, could tell the committee that in a certain district of this county where there is no schoolhouse, a philanthropic individual told the inhabitants that if they would get out a frame and provide the boards, he would at his own expense provide nails, glass, locks, and the necessary materials for finishing a schoolhouse. What was the result? They did get out the frame and raised it, and when I and the honourable chairman had occasion to visit that part of the county together, we enquired why they did not go on and finish it. The worthy individual who had made the proposition, and bought and had in his house the materials for finishing the building, told us that the inhabitants of the district would not find the boards, and, in consequence of that, the erection of the schoolhouse had not been gone on with. A gentleman now present (I will not mention names, as the chairman might blush) offered to give them the boards from a neighbouring mill if they would go and fetch them, but even this they would not do. Although everything was to be had without money, there was no one who felt [90] interest enough in the education of their children to go and bring them to the spot—and to this day the frame stands, as it then did, a melancholy monument of the dreadful apathy which is sometimes to be found even in this comparatively intelligent county."

Mr. Wilmot lived long enough to see a free school system in force in his native province, although he had no share in bringing this result about. Yet that his views on this subject were sound and far in advance of his time is shown by a speech which he made at the time of the opening of the first exhibition in the province in 1852. He said:

"It is unpardonable that any child should grow up in our country without the benefit of, at least, a common-school education. It is the right of the child. It is the duty not only of the parent but of the people; the property of the country should educate the country. All are interested in the diffusion of that intelligence which conserves the peace and promotes the well-being of society. The rich man is interested in proportion to his riches, and should contribute most to the maintenance of schools. Though God has given me no child of my own to educate, I feel concerned for the education of the children of those who do possess them. I feel concerned in what so intimately touches the best interests of our common country. I want to hear the tax collector for schools calling at my [91] door. I want the children of the poor in the remote settlements to receive the advantages now almost confined to their more fortunate brethren and sisters of the towns. I know full well that God has practised no partiality in the distribution of the noblest of his gifts—the intellect; I know that in many a retired hamlet of our province—amid many a painful scene of poverty and toil—there may be found young minds ardent and ingenious and as worthy of cultivation as those of the pampered children of our cities. It is greatly important to the advancement of the country that these should be instructed."

MONEY VOTES

The initiation of money grants by the executive, and the responsibility of the latter to the people, are the two corner-stones on which responsible government must rest. From the very first, Wilmot was an earnest advocate of both these measures; but, owing to the apathy of the people and the disinclination of the members of the legislature to give up what they considered their privileges, it was a difficult matter to accomplish these objects. A reference to the journals of the legislature will show that on numerous occasions he pressed these subjects on the attention of the House of Assembly, and he was ably assisted by his colleague from the county of York, Mr. Charles Fisher, who deserves a foremost place among the men who should be honoured for their efforts to bring about responsible government in the colonies [92] of British North America. It was a peculiar feature in the struggle for responsible government in New Brunswick that, before it ended, the opposition to it came not so much from the British government as from the members of the provincial legislature. It was evident that the system of appropriating money which existed in the House of Assembly was one which was wrong in principle and resulted in getting the province into debt, because there was no guiding hand to control the expenditure. The transfer of the casual and territorial revenues to the provincial treasury in 1837 had placed a very large sum, amounting to about £150,000, at the disposal of the legislature, but this sum was speedily dissipated; and in the year 1842, when Sir William Colebrooke became lieutenant-governor of the province, its finances were in an embarrassed condition.

Towards the close of 1841, a despatch was received from Lord Stanley, the colonial secretary, suggesting that it was desirable that a better system of appropriating the funds of the province should be inaugurated. This brought up a discussion in the legislature during the session of 1842 in regard to the propriety of adopting the principle of placing the initiation of money grants in the executive council. Mr. Wilmot moved a resolution in committee of the whole House "that no appropriation of public money should be made at any future session in supply, for any purpose whatever, [93] until there be a particular account of the income and expenditure of the previous year, together with an estimate of the sums required to be expended, as well for ordinary as extraordinary services, respectively, and also a particular estimate of the principal amount of revenue for the ensuing year." To this an amendment was moved by Mr. Partelow that "Whereas the present mode of appropriation, tested by an experience of more than fifty years, has not only given satisfaction to the people of this province, but repeatedly attracted the deserved approbation of the colonial ministers as securing its constitutional position to every branch of the legislature, therefore resolved, as the opinion of this committee, that it is not expedient to make any alteration in the same." This amendment was carried by a vote of eighteen to twelve.

AN ABUSE UPHELD

Such an amendment as that passed by the House of Assembly of New Brunswick in 1842 would now only be an object of ridicule, because, as a matter of fact, the financial condition of the province showed that the system of appropriation which prevailed was based on false principles, while the alleged approval of the colonial ministers of which so much account was made, had been extended to the most illiberal features of the constitution. There was, however, some excuse for the reluctance of the members of the House of Assembly to surrender the initiation of money votes to the executive, because the executive council [94] of that day was not a body properly under the control of the legislature, or in sympathy with the people.

When the House met in 1843, it was seen that the friends of responsible government were still in the minority. Yet they brought up the subject of the appropriation of the public moneys by a resolution which sought to fix the responsibility of the expenditure on the government. This was met by an amendment moved by Mr. J. W. Weldon, that the House would not surrender the initiation of the money votes. The amendment was carried by a vote of twenty-four to seven, which showed that the friends of Reform had still much leeway to make up before they could hope to impress their views upon the legislature.

SPEECH ON APPROPRIATIONS

As it was hopeless to expect that a House of Assembly thus constituted would vote in favour of the transfer of the initiation of money grants to the executive, Wilmot did not bring up the subject again during the remainder of its term; but by the operation of the Quadrennial Act, which came into force in 1846, a new House was elected in that year, which was largely made up of the same members as the previous one, and at the first session of this House, held early in 1847, Wilmot, during the discussion of the revenue bill, brought up the question of the initiation of money grants in a vigorous and characteristic speech. He said: [95] —

"Can my honourable gentlemen tell me within five thousand pounds of the money asked for, or required for the present session? No, they cannot, and here we are going on in the old way, voting money in the dark, with a thing for our guide called an 'estimate'—a sort of dark lantern with which we are to grope our way through the mazes of legislation. Where is the honourable member for Gloucester who talked so much about the good old rules of our forefathers? I am opposed to the present principle of voting away money; it is, in fact, but giving to tax and taxing to give, this way and that way—every stratagem is used which can be invented in order to carry favourite grants, and thus we proceed from day to day by this system of combination and unprincipled collusion. [Cries of 'Order, Order!'] Honourable members may cry order as much as they please, it is true, and I care not who knows it—let it go forth to the country at large. This system is what the honourable and learned member for Gloucester [Mr. End] denominates 'the glorious old principles of our forefathers,' which should be held as dear as life itself. It is not now as in times gone by, when the legislative council and executive council were one, and consequently we cannot now take the initiation of money grants. This left the whole power in the hands of the assembly; and now, with the report of the committee of finance before us, His Excellency's messages, petitions and everything else, [96] there is not one honourable member around these benches can tell me within five thousand pounds of the amount to be asked for, much less within ten thousand pounds of the amount that will be granted during the present session; and yet, here we are in committee of ways and means for raising a revenue. But it will never answer to have too much information upon this point—if we knew exactly how far we could go and no farther—I perhaps would lose my grant, or another honourable member might lose a grant; this is the system that is pursued. I have held a seat here for twelve years and know the 'ropes' pretty well."

In the following year there was another discussion on the initiation of money grants, arising out of a despatch which had been received from Earl Grey, then colonial minister, in which he referred to the laxity of the system by which money was voted in the New Brunswick legislature without any estimate, and suggested that the initiation of money grants should be surrendered to the executive. This proposal was fiercely opposed, and all the forces of ancient Toryism were rallied against it, one member from Queens County, Mr. Thomas Gilbert, going so far as to apply to the advocacy of the old rotten system the soul-stirring words contained in Nelson's last signal at Trafalgar, "England expects that every man this day will do his duty."

END'S RESOLUTION

In 1850, the last year that Mr. Wilmot sat in the House of Assembly, the matter came up again on [97] a resolution moved by a private member. This was met by an amendment moved by Mr. End, of Gloucester, in the following words:—

"Whereas, the right of originating money grants is inherent in the representatives of the people who are constitutionally responsible to their constituents for the due and faithful user of that right; therefore,

"*Resolved*, As the opinion of this House, that the surrender of such right would amount to a dereliction of public duty and ought not to be entertained by the House of Assembly."

This was carried by a vote of sixteen to eleven. The three members of the government who sat in the House, one of whom was Mr. Wilmot, who had joined it in May 1848, voted with the minority. It was not until the year 1856 that a resolution was passed by the House of Assembly conceding to the executive the right of initiating money grants, and this was carried by a majority of only two in a full House. The first estimate of income and expenditure framed by a New Brunswick government was not laid before the House of Assembly until the session of 1857.

[99]

72

CHAPTER VIII
THE DEMAND FOR RESPONSIBLE GOVERNMENT

When Mr. Wilmot first entered the House of Assembly, many of the members were office-holders and therefore depended on the goodwill of the governor for their positions. At the session of 1842, a bill was introduced for the purpose of putting an end to this evil, in which it was declared that any member of the House of Assembly who should accept the office of executive councillor or any office of profit or emolument under the Crown should be incapable of taking or holding his seat in the General Assembly while in such office, unless reëlected after acceptance thereof. An amendment was moved to exempt executive councillors who did not hold any office of emolument from the provisions of this section, but it was lost by a close vote. Mr. Wilmot voted for the amendment on the ground that a man who was merely an executive councillor without office, and who received no emolument as such, should not be required to go back to the people for reëlection. The bill, nevertheless, was passed by a full House, but it was disallowed by the home authorities on the ground that it was not in accordance with British precedents. The colonial secretary [100] said, "This Act as actually drawn would therefore seem to establish a principle of great importance as well as novelty—the principle, namely, that the Crown may not select its own confidential advisers from amongst representatives of the people unless the person so chosen should be willing to hazard a new election. How far it is wise to erect such a barrier between the executive government and the popular branch of the legislature would seem to be a matter well meriting serious consideration." In the same despatch, the propriety of seats in the assembly being vacated for the same reasons which would vacate seats in the House of Commons was fully conceded. The stand taken by Wilmot in regard to this subject was therefore the one which was approved by the home government and was further endorsed by subsequent legislation. Yet it was not until 1849 that the Act was passed which finally settled the question, and required members of the legislature accepting office to vacate their seats in the House of Assembly and go back to their constituents for reëlection.

THE GOVERNOR CENSURED

Sir William Colebrooke had not been a popular governor since the appointment of his son-in-law to the office of provincial secretary. The House of Assembly, therefore, was disposed to watch his conduct very closely and to criticize actions which perhaps would not have attracted so much attention under other conditions. During the session of 1846, it was shown that he had appropriated a portion of [101] the surplus civil list fund, amounting to about three thousand pounds, for the purpose of defraying the expenses of surveying Crown lands in Madawaska. [6] This money was taken by the order of the colonial secretary, Lord Stanley. Thus it appeared that, although the province was supposed to have the control of the territorial revenue, the British government assumed the right to dispose of a portion of this revenue without the consent or authority of the House of Assembly. The conduct of the governor in connection with this matter was censured in a strongly worded resolution which was passed by the House of Assembly almost unanimously. [7] The time had gone by when the [102] representative of the Crown could do as he liked with the public funds of the province, as had been the case in former years.

The legislature was dissolved in 1846 under the provisions of the Act which limited its term to four years. On the last day of the session Wilmot bade farewell to the members of the House, and stated that he did not intend to offer himself again for reëlection. No doubt he was quite sincere in making this statement at the time, but he soon had reason to change his mind. The people of the county of York were unwilling to lose the services of the champion of their rights in the House of Assembly, so that he found it necessary to consent to be again nominated. He was returned at the head of the poll, and with him Mr. Charles Fisher, who had been his colleague in two previous legislatures.

The general election of 1846 brought a considerable number of new men into the House, and in point of liberality the new assembly was a slight improvement on its predecessor. The legislature met near the end of January in the following year. The government at that time consisted of only five persons, of whom two were members of the House of Assembly and three of the legislative council. It appeared that negotiations had been going on with some of the members of the Opposition for the purpose of filling up the vacancies in the executive council. Wilmot had been offered a seat in that [103] body, but made it a condition of his acceptance that he should go in with two of his friends, provided the council was filled up to the number of seven, or three, if filled up to the number of nine. This was not agreed to, so he remained outside the government. During the first week of the session three new members were added to the government, one of them being the surveyor-general, Mr. Baillie, who had been elected a member of the House of Assembly for the county of York. The arrangements made were not satisfactory to Wilmot and his friends, and the government had to face what was practically a want of confidence resolution. It was moved by Mr. Fisher and was as follows:—

"*Resolved*, As the opinion of this House, that while it fully recognizes the accountability of the executive council to the assembly, it will expect that henceforth the provincial administration will, from time to time, prepare and bring before the legislature such measures as may be required for the development of the provincial resources and the general advancement of the public interests."

ASSAILS THE GOVERNMENT

In the course of the debate Wilmot spoke with great power and effect. The following report of his speech on that occasion may serve to convey to the reader some idea of his manner and method as a public speaker:—

"The honourable gentleman might have spared himself the trouble of making the defence he did. I have heard that he was to be presented with a [104] gold medal for his admirable defence of that nearly extinct race—the old Family Compact. I see that I shall have to cross a lance with my honourable and learned friend [Mr. Hazen] politically. Yet I hope the same good feeling which has characterized the debate thus far will be continued. A great deal has been said about politics and political principles, but my political principles are not of yesterday—I have gleaned them from the history of my country, a country which we are all proud to own. Will any honourable member dare to tell me that because we are three thousand miles from the heart of the British empire the blood of freemen shall not flow through the veins of the sons of New Brunswick? If so, I have yet to learn the reason. Before I sit down I will endeavour to show my honourable friends what the distinction is between Liberals and Conservatives — what the Liberals have done, and what the Conservatives have not done. Now to the resolution. My honourable friend said yesterday that the resolution meant initiation of money grants. When this announcement was made I heard a shout from the direction of my honourable friend, Mr. Partelow, in a tenor voice, and an honourable member in the rear [Mr. Barberie] joining in a sort of falsetto accompaniment. I think my honourable friend [Mr. Hazen] is much to blame for having accused his honourable colleague [Mr. Woodward] with writing an article in a city paper. What, suppose he did write [105] SPEECH ON REFORMit, do not some of the first noblemen and statesmen in England write for the papers? I will not deny that I have written for the papers myself some little squibs. But it is wrong to place an honourable member in the position where he will have to affirm or deny it. A great cry has been raised of a contemplated attack on the government, and, after all, it has turned out that their fears have been excited by a newspaper paragraph. The government has fortified all their outposts, and His Excellency and two aides have been on the lookout for the coming attack. At length my honourable colleague [Mr. Fisher] brought forth his resolutions when they said to each other, 'Why, this doesn't mean anything; there is no attack.' But they slept over it one night, cracked some wine upon it, and while sitting under the mahogany they said — 'Hazen, there is something in these resolutions of Fisher's, depend upon it — some hidden meaning — what shall we say it is? what will we call it? we must give them some ugly name, or they will pass.' 'Oh,' said Hazen, 'I have it — initiation of money grants — that'll do; I'll just go down to the House and cry out "mad dog," "initiation of money grants"; members will become alarmed, and we'll succeed in defeating them.' But the honourable member from St. John [Mr. Jordan] has made the most wonderful discoveries; he has taken a peep from the lookout station at the enemy; he has looked through a political microscope, [106] and has discovered more than the commander-in-chief himself. 'Why,' says he, 'there's everything there — I see "free trade" and "protection" both, and let me see — I — there's the "Board of Works," too; and round on the other side I see "Municipal Corporations."' I will endeavour before I sit down to prove that the arguments of my honourable friend Mr. Hazen are fallacious. He has been developing at a great rate yesterday; he was not asked to develop the money, but to bring down such measures as would develop the provincial resources; this is the meaning of the resolution, and, had not my honourable friend become alarmed for the safety of the government, there is no man into whose hands I would sooner place the resolution. But he has chosen to put the construction upon the resolution which he has done, and other honourable members said, 'Oh, he knows what it means better than I do; he has cried "mad dog" and we'll follow him.' The government is not asked to bring in the revenue bill, or any other bill which involves the principle of money grants. All the resolution requires is, that they shall be prepared, at the opening of the session, with such measures as may be considered for the general welfare of the country, and not keep the assembly waiting two or three weeks for the motion of the government, as has been the case this session. Honourable members will recollect that there is a constituency behind them to whom they are accountable; but [107] they may resolve and re-resolve as they please. There is a spirit of inquiry abroad among the people, a political intelligence, which was not to be found a few years since when my honourable friend denounced responsible government as all nonsense! What was the case when responsible government was first talked of in this province? Who descended from their lofty eminence to warn the people to beware of these new doctrines? The old official Family Compact party — they who entrenched themselves behind the prerogative of the Crown in 1836, came down to the people and said, 'We who have done so much for you — we who have watched over and guarded you, beware of that dreadful monster, responsible government.' These are the people who call themselves Conservatives. What, I would ask, did they conserve? Everything but the good of the country; and, had the Conservatism of 1836 been carried out, an insulted people would ere this have risen in their majesty and would have shaken off the yoke of bondage under which they had been labouring.

RESPONSIBLE GOVERNMENT

"It has been said by honourable members of the government that there is no distinction between Liberals and Conservatives. If this is the case, why did they object to have me and two others take seats in the council because we were Liberals? Here is a question which I would like my honourable friends to answer. The Conservatives do not wish to see any power in the hands of the people. [108] [Interjection from Mr. End—'Not too much.'] The honourable member from Gloucester, Mr. End, has receded from his principles wonderfully; his speech yesterday was certainly a most extraordinary one. He said to the government in a most supplicating tone of voice, 'Give me fair play—give me the appointment of all the bye-road commissioners, magistrates, sheriffs, and so on, in Gloucester, and I will support you; that is all I want.' I will take care not to be misunderstood in these matters, I will not allow any man to be the exponent of my political principles. I believe departmental government to be inseparable from our institutions, but will oppose the immediate introduction of the whole system; I will bring it in step by step as the country is prepared for it. Some extraordinary notions are entertained as to the source from whence the power of the government is derived; the freedom of government does not come down from the Crown, it goes up from the people; and if the people are fit for these institutions they are fit for self-government. I have frequently said that they who get the people's money shall do the people's work. [From Mr. Partelow—'Yes, that's right.'] I will now come down a step further—what was the case in 1837? I am not going to disclose any secrets this time—but will speak low. I wish to ask my honourable friend [Mr. Hazen] if, after the administration changed in 1837, the government had the cordial coöperation of the heads of departments? No! [109] THE PEOPLE SUPREMEThere has been a counterworking going on—a constant endeavour to lead the government astray and place them in a wrong position, and my generoushearted friend [Mr. Hazen] has to come down to this House and defend them. It is a political fact, that previous to 1841 the heads of departments in this province were in open hostility to the government. [From Mr. End—'They could do no harm.'] If the departmental system were in operation, and their tenure of office depended upon their ability so to conduct the government as to merit the confidence of the assembly and the people, there would be none of this stabbing in the dark, and running off the track. It is, in my opinion, the only constitutional remedy for the good working of the government. These five gentlemen who have lately formed the mixed government, asked for departmental government when they signed the address to the queen; yet now they refuse to adopt it. I should like to know when they intend to graduate—does it depend upon the age of the country or the state of the atmosphere? The fact is, whenever the people of this country, through their representatives, choose to ask for it they must get it. In 1844 they ran to the rescue of the prerogative in Canada; but the very next year the same case came down to their own doors! The tune was changed then, and an address was prepared to the queen signed by the whole assembly except five. Why is this brought about—why is the tune changed so suddenly? [110] They at first said responsible government is not fit for a colony—the next cry was, it is not fit for New Brunswick, and finally they said, when they addressed the queen—we must have it. Mr. Roebuck called upon Lord John Russell to explain what responsible government was, which he has done [reads the speech as delivered in the British parliament], and, when they had first asked for it here, it was in full operation in Canada. My honourable friend [Mr. Hazen] has accused me of having receded; but I will now ask him to point out how I have done so? He has also said that I was brought forward at the last election by the Conservatives. True, but I was backed by all my old friends, and I told them if they took me, they must do so with all my former opinions—opinions which I never will give up. When they talk about there being no difference in political names,—there is a difference; those who have contended for Liberal principles have their names covered with obloquy. We ask for a constitution that, while it protects the queen upon the throne, throws, at the same time, its paternal arms around the helpless infant. This we ask for, this we want—the pure, the free, the glorious constitution of England; for this we have contended, for this the Liberals of New Brunswick have fought, and let them call us rebels who have nothing else to write about, I care not; we ask for a system that will give fair play to all—that will upset all Family Compacts, and give to the sons of [111] New Brunswick their birthright, the benefit of free institutions and self-government. This is what we want, and I will not submit tamely to be called a rebel; I defy any honourable member to look at my political life and say where I have overstepped the bounds of the constitution? If I do live three thousand miles from the great body of the empire, still that empire sends its blood through the veins of every British subject. A son of New Brunswick has the same right to the benefit of her institutions as has a resident of London, and I will not submit to be cut off by any political manœuvring."

REFORM DEFEATED

After a long debate, Mr. Fisher's resolution was defeated by a vote of twenty-three to twelve, which showed that the friends of Reform had still much work to do.

FOOTNOTES:

[6] This occurred during the time of the "rump" government composed of Messrs. Simonds, Allen and McLeod, the members of the executive who refused to resign at the time of the Reade appointment.

[7] The following resolutions which were moved by Mr. Partelow were carried in the House of Assembly by a vote of twenty to two:

"1st. *Resolved*, That this committee deeply regret that His Excellency the lieutenant-governor in council should not have felt himself authorized to communicate to the House the despatch of the Right Honourable the Secretary of State for the Colonies, of January 5th, 1845, relative to the appropriation of the surplus civil list, in answer to the address of the House of Assembly of March 14th, 1845, whereby the House was prevented from representing, by an humble and dutiful address to Her Majesty, that such appropriation was not in accordance with the despatch of the Right Honourable the Secretary of State for the Colonies of August 31st, 1836.

"2d. *Resolved*, As the opinion of this committee, that any funds necessary to carry out the fourth article of the Treaty of Washington, being a national treaty with a foreign power, ought not to be chargeable upon the funds of this province; and that the House should, by an humble and dutiful address to Her Majesty, pray that any appropriation made for that purpose from the surplus civil list fund may be refunded to the same."

[113]

CHAPTER IX
THE VICTORY IS WON

The session of 1848 was destined to be a memorable one in the history of responsible government in New Brunswick. It was evident that with the House as then constituted no progress could be made unless a change were brought about in the views of some of its members by outside pressure. In this instance the pressure came from the imperial government, which desired to bring the political condition of New Brunswick into line with that of Canada and Nova Scotia. In March, 1847, Earl Grey, the colonial secretary, addressed a despatch to Sir John Harvey, the governor of Nova Scotia, in which he laid down the principles which he thought should control colonial administration. The most important feature of this despatch was its declaration with reference to the composition of the executive council. With regard to office-holders in general, Earl Grey thought that they ought not to be disturbed in consequence of any change of government, but he was of opinion that a different rule should apply to such officials as were members of the executive council. On this point he adopted the language of Mr. Poulett Thomson (Lord Sydenham), who, in a despatch to Lord [114] John Russell, written at Halifax, in the year 1840, said: —

"The functions of the executive council, on the other hand, are, it is perfectly clear, of a totally different character; they are a body upon whom the governor must be able to call at any or at all times for advice, with whom he can consult upon the measures to be submitted to the legislature, and in whom he may find instruments within its walls to introduce such amendments in the laws as he may think necessary, or to defend his acts and his policy. It is obvious, therefore, that those who compose this body must be persons whose constant attendance on the governor can be secured; principally, therefore, officers of the government, but, when it may be expedient to introduce others, men holding seats in one or other House, taking a leading part in political life, and above all, exercising influence over the assembly.

"The last, and in my opinion by far the most serious, defect in the government is the utter absence of power in the executive, and its total want of energy to attempt to occupy the attention of the country upon real improvements, or to lead the legislature in the preparation and adoption of measures for the benefit of the colony. It does not appear to have occurred to any one that it is one of the first duties of the government to suggest improvements where they are wanted; that, the constitution having placed the power of legislation [115] in the hands of an assembly and a council, it is only by acting through these bodies that the duty can be performed; and that, if these proper and legitimate functions of government are neglected, the necessary result must be not only that the improvements which the people have a right to expect will be neglected, and the prosperity of the country checked, but that each branch of legislature will misuse its power, and the popular mind be easily led into excitement upon mere abstract theories of government to which their attention is directed as the remedy for the uneasiness they feel."

He concluded by expressing the opinion that the peculiar circumstances of Nova Scotia presented no insuperable obstacle to the immediate adoption of that system of parliamentary government which had long prevailed in the mother country.

A MEMORABLE DESPATCH

A copy of this despatch was sent to the lieutenant-governor of New Brunswick and it was laid before the House in pursuance of an address which had been passed a few days before. It was understood that the principles laid down in this despatch would be equally applicable to the province of New Brunswick, and Mr. Fisher moved that the House should approve of them and of their application to New Brunswick. This resolution was carried by a vote of twenty-four to eleven, which was a complete reversal of the vote of the previous session. Among those who voted for the resolution [116] were the three members of the government who had seats in the House of Assembly and who had been previously opposed to any such change in the political system of the country. Thus the victory for responsible government was practically won, and it only remained to perfect the details.

Immediately after the prorogation of the legislature, a reorganization of the government took place, Messrs. Baillie, Shore and Johnston retired and their places were taken by Messrs. Wilmot, Partelow, Fisher and Kinnear. Mr. Wilmot became attorney-general in the place of Mr. Peters, recently deceased, who had filled that office for twenty years. Mr. Partelow became provincial secretary in place of John Simcoe Saunders. Mr. Kinnear, who had been made solicitor-general in 1846, now became a member of the government under the new system, while Mr. Fisher took his seat as a member of the government without office. Thus were the principles of responsible government vindicated and established in New Brunswick. The provincial secretary, the attorney-general and the solicitor-general became political officers subject to change with every change of government. The surveyor-general, Mr. Baillie, by resigning from the government escaped this condition for the time being, but it was not long before that office also became political, Mr. Baillie himself retiring with a pension in 1851. [117]

INFLUENCE OF COLONIAL OFFICE

Messrs. Wilmot and Fisher were much censured by their friends for becoming members of a government that was essentially Conservative and in which they were in a minority. But as the principles for which they had contended had been admitted and were now in a measure established, there seemed to be no reason why they should not assist in working them out. Wilmot as attorney-general certainly had greater opportunities of advancing the cause of Reform than as a private member, and he and Fisher working together were able to exercise a strong influence on the administration. In the following year, as has already been seen, a measure was carried voiding the seats of members of the assembly who became heads of departments in the government, or enjoyed any office of profit or emolument under the Crown, and this was all that was necessary to establish responsible government on a firm basis. There was indeed one other difficulty, the interference of the colonial office and the influence of the governor, who had been accustomed to govern the province largely by means of despatches. This influence was one which could only be got rid of by degrees, for the wise men of Downing Street always thought they knew much better what colonists required than did the colonists themselves. The colonial secretary undertook to dictate to the province as to the kind of tariff it should pass, and to refuse assent to the passage of bills by the legislature giving a preference to [118] any particular county or granting bounties to fishermen or others engaged in any special calling. It was felt to be a hardship that the province was not permitted to give encouragement to any industry which it desired to assist, and so strong was this feeling that at the session of 1850, immediately after the receipt of a despatch from Earl Grey disallowing the bill of the previous session granting bounties for the cultivation of hemp, a bill was introduced and carried by an overwhelming majority in the assembly appropriating three thousand pounds for bounties to fishermen. This bill was rejected by the council, so that the colonial secretary was spared the difficulty which would have been involved in being defied by the New Brunswick legislature. It was also felt to be a great hardship that, at a time when the colonies were being deprived of the preferential tariff they had so long enjoyed in the English markets, they should be debarred from entering into commercial arrangements with foreign nations. A series of strongly worded resolutions on this subject was moved by Mr. David Wark, and was well supported, although not carried. The language used by many of the speakers during the debate showed that the loyal feelings which had always distinguished the people of the province were being subjected to a severe strain by the policy of the British government. These interferences with provincial rights continued for many years after Wilmot had retired from [119] public life, and therefore it is unnecessary to refer to them further.

THE PORTLAND CONVENTION

Wilmot had but few opportunities during his active career as a public man of displaying his abilities outside of his native province. His fame as an orator was therefore mainly a local one, and the Portland Railway Convention of 1850 was the first occasion on which he was recognized as one of the best speakers on the continent. That great gathering of the railway and business men of the United States and Canada was assembled for the purpose of taking measures to secure a shorter ocean route to Europe than was afforded by steamships sailing from New York. It was thought that a better plan would be to run steamships from some port on the west coast of Ireland to a port on the east coast of Nova Scotia, a distance of about two thousand miles, and to connect the latter with New York by a line of railway. No one doubted at that time that this was a plan that was likely to succeed, and probably it would have done

so if there had been no improvement in the construction of steamships. No one dreamed in those days that boats with a speed of
twenty-five knots an hour and of twenty thousand tons displace-
ment would be running to New York before the century was ended,
and that the voyage to Liverpool would be reduced to less than six
days.

The Portland Convention included many eminent men from the
United States and Canada and not [120] a few that could justly be
described as orators, but it was universally admitted that in eloquence Attorney-General Wilmot, of New Brunswick, exceeded
them all. The reporter of the proceedings of the convention stated,
in the pamphlet afterwards published, that it was due to the speaker and to himself to say that "he had been entirely unable to give
anything like a report of the remarks of Mr. Wilmot." The reporter
also quotes the statement of another that "Mr. Wilmot delivered one
of the most spicy, eloquent and enlivening speeches which he ever
heard, which, while it kept the audience in the best spirits, was
replete with noble sentiments commending themselves to the hearts
of all present. His remarks were generally upon the moral, social
and intellectual influences which would result from the contemplated work. No sketch would do justice to its power and beauty, its
flashes of wit and humour."

WILMOT'S GREAT SPEECH

The following report of Wilmot's great convention speech, although admittedly very imperfect, is given as almost the only example that survives of his eloquence: —

"I find myself in a new position in addressing a convention in a
city, in a state, and under a government that is foreign to me, as far
as citizenship is concerned. But I feel myself at home, for I am
among those who derive their inheritance from the same common
ancestry. I am, Mr. President, not a son of New England, but a
grandson, and I can [121] find the old gravestone which indicates
the graves of my ancestors, in a pleasant village of Connecticut
[cheers].

"We in the provinces came to this convention at your call. We
have responded to your invitation and you have given us a brother's welcome. Physiologists affirm that the exercise of the muscles

tends to their enlargement and fuller development; and phrenologists affirm that the exercise of the different faculties develops in a corresponding degree the bumps upon the cranium. I would beg to add something to this category,—the exercise of benevolence and kindness enlarges the heart, and since I have been among you I have felt my heart growing big within me [cheers].

"I am delighted to see this day, and could I give expression to the emotions which swell up within me I would do so, but my power fails in the attempt, and I cannot presume to make a speech. We do not, however, meet to consult about California, where one hundred and twelve hour speeches are necessary, or about the admission of New Mexico into the Union. Our object is to effect an admission into the great railroad union, and on this question we admit of no 'compromises.' We go straight ahead in our purpose and the union will be effected [cheers].

"I know, Mr. President, it is a great work in which we are engaged. I know that it looks vast, if not impossible of achievement to those who [122] have not studied its relations and its details, but those who look at it through the enlarged medium which its contemplation presents will find that difficulties diminish as its importance grows upon their vision.

"Look at the progress of similar enterprises among yourselves in the state of Maine, and other parts of New England, and then say whether anything is required of us but union of effort and faith in the result of our exertions. In prosecuting our work in this matter, we must have faith; but as faith without works is dead, let us put forth our exertions and go steadily forward to a speedy and glorious completion of our great enterprise [cheers].

"If the timid falter and the doubting hold back, there are others who will take their places and keep our ranks full. We have only to hold our position, and drive back the army of doubters, or opposers, who may resist our march. We must give them the same reception that General Taylor gave to the army of Santa Anna at Buena Vista. If opposed by superior numbers, or if on any part of the field there are those who hesitate, or hold back when a stronghold of the enemy is to be carried, I would repeat the order of General Taylor: 'A little more grape, Captain Poor' [8] [tremendous cheers].

"It is written in the decrees of eternal Providence, [123] Mr. President, that we shall learn war no more; we may then go on side by side with glorious emulation for the cause of virtue and philanthropy throughout the world, striving who shall out-vie the other. How changed in every respect, now, is the condition of our race! How glorious the sight of two great peoples uniting as one, 'to draw more closely the bands of brotherhood, that yet shall make of all mankind but one great brotherhood of nations.' The sentiment of that resolution which embodies this idea is worthy of its author and of the American character; but it is also a sentiment to which the people of the British empire will respond [cheers].

"Sir, I found in the circular which invited us here this sentiment expressed, in terms which aroused to the fullest enthusiasm the mind of every man in the British provinces: 'The spirit of peace has at last prevailed—national animosities, sectional and political hostility have disappeared between the English races since the establishment of the boundaries of Maine and Oregon, and the contests of war have been succeeded by a noble and generous rivalry for the promotion of the arts of peace. The introduction of the steamship and the railway has made former enemies friends. National hostility has given way to commercial and social intercourse, and under whatever form of government they may hereafter exist, they can never again become hostile or unfriendly' [cheers]. [124]

"To this sentiment I respond with all my heart. It is this sentiment that has brought us together. I know not who was the author of this circular, but whoever he may be, in the name of every Englishman—in the name of every American, sir, in the name of humanity, I tender him thanks [cheers].

"An enterprise aiming to accomplish such results, and which is in and of itself calculated to produce such results, cannot fail of success. The whole civilized world is interested in its accomplishment. There are some good old-fashioned people who think we are going too fast and too far in our railroad enterprises. We have, they say, lived and got along well enough without railroads, and now you seem to think that your temporal salvation depends upon it! Blot out your telegraphs, lay up your steamboats,—what darkness would come upon the world! We must form ourselves into a council of war for the purpose of combating these old prejudices, and, instead of being turned away from our objects, we will take stronger grounds than ever occupied before.

"Mr. President, we of the provinces have made up our minds no longer to remain quiet in our present condition. With all the fine natural advantages our country possesses, we make comparatively slow progress, and our province itself is scarcely known to the world. I shall be pardoned here for relating an anecdote to illustrate the truth of this remark. [125]

"In a recent visit to Washington upon official business, I had occasion to tarry a few days in the city of New York, and among the places that I visited with a friend was one of the colleges in the city. My friend introduced me to a learned professor as his friend, the 'Attorney-general of New Brunswick.' We entered into conversation on a variety of subjects, and he inquired when I came over to the city, and as to various matters going on in the neighbouring state. Seeing the mistake of the learned professor, I thought it hardly kind to mortify him by correcting it, and I answered in the best way I could, and took my leave; and to this hour, I suppose, the learned professor thinks he was talking with the attorney-general of the fine old state of New Jersey [tremendous cheers].

"Seeing that my own country itself was hardly known beyond its bounds, I felt a little concern that she should not always remain in this condition. I felt, as many of my friends and neighbours have long felt, that we must look at home for the means of making our province honoured and respected abroad. And we intend to open this line of railway entirely across the breadth of our province and bring ourselves into connection with the world [cheers].

"Mr. President, I cannot omit, in this connection, the expression of my profound regard for the American Union. It is the union of these states that has given you greatness and strength at home [126] and the respect and admiration of the civilized world [long-continued cheers].

"The great interests of Christianity, of philanthropy and of liberty, throughout the world, depend upon the union of these states. We of New Brunswick, of Nova Scotia, and of Canada are deeply interested in its existence. If there is any question of the day that interests us more than all others, it is this very question of the perpetuity of the union. For myself, I think there should be passed a law providing that the man who would even conceive the idea of a dissolution of the union should be guilty of treason. In the sincerity of my heart, I say, perish the man who should dare to think of it [tremendous cheers]!"

With respect to railway legislation Wilmot was not in advance of many others in the province whose general political views were less liberal than his own. There was always a good deal of local feeling injected into the discussion of railway matters and Wilmot, who was a resident of Fredericton, incurred a good deal of censure for the ridicule which he threw on the proposal to build a railway from St. John to Shediac, which is now a part of the Intercolonial. As this railway brought the counties bordering on the Straits of Northumberland and the Gulf of St. Lawrence into easy communication with St. John, nothing is more clear than that of all the railways then projected in the province it was the one most likely to be useful and [127] profitable, but Wilmot apparently could not forget the fact that it did not touch his own county. His speech on this subject was made in the legislature before the meeting of the Portland Convention, and it is worthy of note that five-sixths of the Shediac Railway was to be used as part of the magnificent European and North American Railway scheme which was so much lauded by him in his Portland speech.

HIS WORK IN LEGISLATION

There is not much to be said in regard to the political life of Wilmot after he became attorney-general. His principal legislative achievement while he filled that office was an Act for the consolidation of the criminal law with regard to the definition of certain indictable offences and the punishment thereof. This was a useful but not a brilliant work, which many another man might have performed equally well. In the session of 1850, Wilmot carried a bill through the House of Assembly for the reduction of the salaries of the judges of the supreme court and some other officials, but this measure did not pass the legislative council. He had always been in favour of a low scale of salaries as best suited to the conditions which prevailed in the province. The scale had been fixed in 1836, when the casual and territorial revenues were placed under the control of the province, but an agitation soon afterwards commenced for further reductions. The imperial government would not consent to the reduction of any salary while the [128] holder of the office lived, except in the case of the surveyor-general, whose duties had been decreased, but it agreed to a lower scale for future occupants of the offices. In this way the salary of the provincial secretary had been reduced from £1,599 11s. to £600; that of the surveyor-general from £2,019 4s. 4d. to £1,209 12s. 4d., and that of the auditor-general from £500 to £346 3s. The salaries of the judges, however, remained the same in 1850 as they had been in 1836, viz., £1,096 3s. for the chief-justice and £750 for each of the puisne judges. Wilmot's bill reduced these salaries to £700 for the chief-justice and £600 to each of the other judges. He also voted for a resolution in favour of making the legislative council elective, and that an address should be presented to Her Majesty asking her to consent to the passage of such a bill. A favourable answer was received from Her Majesty, but the scheme to make the legislative council elective was never carried into effect, in consequence of the opposition which it encountered in that body.

There is no doubt that the popularity of Wilmot seriously declined after he entered the government. This was very plainly seen at the general election which took place in June, 1850, when he narrowly escaped defeat, being the lowest on the poll of the members elected, while his colleague in the government, Mr. Fisher, was defeated, polling less than one-half the number of votes given to the candidate who was highest on the poll. But, on the whole, [129] the result throughout the province was favourable to the cause of Reform, and among those elected in York who stood higher on the poll than Wilmot were two new members who held advanced views with respect to the amendment of the constitution.

THE GOVERNOR AND THE JUDGES

Although responsible government had been conceded to New Brunswick, and it was admitted that public offices should be bestowed in accordance with the wishes of the people, the close of Wilmot's legislative career was marked by an event which showed that the old order of things had not entirely passed away. Chief-

Justice Chipman, owing to failing health, resigned his seat on the bench in the autumn of 1850, and it became necessary to provide for a successor. A meeting of the executive council was called for the purpose of filling the vacancy, and six members of the council out of the eight who were present signed a memorandum to the effect that it was not advisable to appoint any person to the vacant office, but that such a division of the work of the judiciary should be made by the legislature as would secure the efficient discharge of the judicial duties by three judges, together with the Master of the Rolls. Wilmot was one of the persons who signed this memorandum, but on the following day he called on the governor and asked that his name might be withdrawn from it, he having in the meantime apparently changed his mind. The governor, Sir Edmund Head, asked the [130] judges whether, in their opinion, three of them would be able to do all the judicial business of the country, and received from them a strongly worded protest against any such alteration in the number of judges. Mr. Fisher, who was one of the members of the executive present at the meeting, submitted to the governor a paper in which he took strong grounds against the proposal to reduce the number of judges. Sir Edmund Head referred the matter to the home authorities, and they decided that the proposed change in the number of judges was not advisable. Moreover, they decided as to who should fill the vacant offices, and asked the governor to appoint Mr. Justice Carter to the position of chief-justice and to offer a puisne judgeship to the attorney-general, Mr. Wilmot, and if he refused it to the solicitor-general, Mr. Kinnear. Mr. Wilmot accepted, and thus brought his political career to an end.

FOOTNOTES:

[8] This is an adaptation of General Taylor's words. John A. Poor was the chief promoter of the European and North American Railway and the chairman of the committee of arrangements of the Portland Convention.

[131]

CHAPTER X
JUDGE AND GOVERNOR

The opinion that was entertained of Mr. Wilmot by those who were closely associated with him in the work of Reform was well expressed by the late Mr. George E. Fenety, in his *Political Notes*.

"A great luminary," says Mr. Fenety, "set in semi-darkness on the day that Mr. Wilmot left the forum for the bench. He was the light of the House for sixteen years, the centre from whence radiated most of the sparkling gems in the political firmament. It was at a time of life (comparatively a young man) and a period when talents such as his were most wanted by his party and his country. Notwithstanding his supposed mistake in having joined a Conservative government, the Liberals were always willing to receive their old leader back with outstretched arms—ready to forgive and go along again with him over the old road, and, to a man, would have held to him had he made a stand against Sir Edmund Head, and told him—'thus far and no farther shalt thou go'."

Many of Wilmot's friends regretted that he should have accepted the office of judge on the conditions under which it was offered. They thought [132] that as attorney-general he was entitled to the position of chief-justice, and that in consenting to take the puisne judgeship he had lowered himself. It is hardly necessary to discuss a question of this kind at the present day. No doubt he had reasons of his own for retiring from the arena of politics. The work he had been doing for the public had placed a great strain upon him and interfered with his legal business to a very serious extent. He was never a wealthy man, and had therefore to consider his own future, while a position on the bench was one of honour and dignity which was regarded as worthy of acceptance by any member of the legal profession.

There was nothing worthy of note in the career of Mr. Wilmot as a judge. He was never considered to be a deeply read lawyer, but he filled the office of judge with dignity and general acceptance. His duties were not sufficiently arduous to prevent him from having leisure to engage in other lines of inquiry, for his mind was much interested in questions connected with science. He frequently appeared on the lecture platform and always with success.

When confederation was accomplished, it was felt that of all the natives of New Brunswick he was the most worthy to be appointed its first lieutenant-governor under the new régime. Judge Wilmot himself was willing to accept the office as a fitting close to his long and active career as a public man; [133] but for some reason, which it is now impossible to ascertain, the appointment was not made until about a year after confederation. Judge Wilmot became lieutenant-governor on July 23rd, 1868, and continued to hold that honourable and important office until November 14th, 1873, when he was succeeded by the Hon. S. L. Tilley.

OTHER ACTIVITIES

So far, we have been considering Wilmot as a politician and member of the legislature, but a very imperfect idea of his character would be gathered from regarding him merely in these capacities. He was a many-sided man, and had other interests which occupied his attention as much as, or more than, those public questions to which he devoted so much of his vigour. It has already been stated that his father was a member of the Baptist Church, and one of the founders of the church of that denomination in Fredericton. It does not appear that the son ever identified himself with that Church, or that while a youth he gave much attention to religious matters. It was not until after the death of his first wife, which took place in 1833, that he became affected by religious influences and began to attend the services of the Methodist Church, the pulpit of which was then filled by the Rev. Enoch Wood, a man of much ability and eloquence whose style of oratory was very impressive. Under his ministrations Mr. Wilmot became a convert, was baptized and joined the Methodist Church in Fredericton, and from that time until the close of his life [134] he was a very prominent figure in it. He filled the office of superintendent of its Sunday School for upwards of twenty-five years, and was the leader of the church choir for thirty years. When he was appointed governor it was thought that he would give up these offices, but he still continued to fill them, and was superintendent of the Sunday School up to the day when his life came to an end. He always took a great interest in questions relating to the Bible, and frequently lectured on topics connected with it. He vehemently opposed the teachings of Darwin and others who followed the same line of inquiry, and he stoutly maintained that wherever the Bible and science were in conflict, science was in the wrong. He seems to have been, from first to last, an unquestioning believer in the doctrines of the Christian religion, and he viewed with great disfavour any one who ventured to question any part of its creed. As a lecturer he was eloquent and though discursive, always interesting. None of his lectures were written, so that to-day they are only a fading memory to those who heard them delivered. Though found acceptable at the time, it is hardly likely that, if delivered at the present day, they would enjoy so high a degree of popularity. People are not now so willing to accept sweeping assertions which are in conflict with the conclusions of scientific men who have devoted their lives to a patient study of the phenomena of life and the records of creation. [135]

INTEREST IN MILITARY MATTERS

One of the most pleasing features of Judge Wilmot's character was his fondness for children. He was never so happy as when among the young people, and long after he became a judge he took an intense interest in drilling the schoolboys and instructing them in all martial exercises; indeed, he seemed to be quite as much devoted to this work as he was to any other of his numerous employments. When a very young man, he became an ensign in the first battalion of York County militia, and speedily rose to be captain. When the so-called Aroostook War [9] broke out in 1839 he was major of a company of rifles attached to that battalion, and he volunteered for active service at the front. His interest in military matters continued [136] until a late period, and, in the first military camp organized in the province by the lieutenant-governor, the Hon. Arthur Gordon, in 1863, he commanded one of the battalions. If Wilmot had not been a politician and a lawyer, he might have been a great evangelist or a great soldier.

Judge Wilmot was very fond of flowers, and the beautiful grounds at Evelyn Grove, where he resided, were looked upon as the finest in the province. Nearly every visitor to Fredericton found his way to that charming place and was sure of a cordial welcome from the judge, who delighted to show strangers what he had been able to accomplish in growing flowers and rare plants. Not the least interesting feature of such visits was the conversation of the host, who abounded in knowledge of horticulture, and was always ready to give others the benefit of his information. It was in this lovely retreat that the last years of Mr. Wilmot's life were passed. When his term as governor expired, the government of Canada very properly gave him a pension as a retired judge. In 1875 he succeeded the Right Hon. Mr. Childers, as second commissioner under the Prince Edward Island Land Purchase Act. He was nominated as one of the arbitrators in the Ontario and North-West Boundary Commission, but did not live long enough to act in that capacity.

HIS DEATH

During the last two or three years of his life he suffered much from chronic neuralgia, which sometimes [137] prevented him from stirring out-of-doors. No serious result was anticipated, and he was generally able to take active exercise and engage in his usual routine of duty. On Monday, May 20th, 1878, while driving in his carriage with his wife, he complained of a sudden and severe pain in the region of the heart. He was at once driven home and a physician summoned, but in a few minutes he passed away. He had not quite completed his seventieth year. His death evoked expressions of regret and sympathy from every part of the province, and tributes of respect and admiration from many who resided in other parts of Canada and in the United States.

Judge Wilmot was twice married. His first wife, whom he married in 1832, was Jane, daughter of Mr. James Balloch, of St. John. She died very soon after their marriage, and in 1834 he married Miss Elizabeth Black, daughter of the Hon. William Black, of Halifax, and granddaughter of the Rev. William Black, who is regarded as the apostle of Wesleyan Methodism in the Maritime Provinces.

In estimating the character and achievements of L. A. Wilmot, regard must be had to the conditions under which the battle for responsible government was fought, and the peculiar difficulties he had to face. He had not only to contend against governors determined to use their power to the utmost, an immovable legislative council and a [138] reactionary executive, but he had to attempt to inspire with something of his own spirit a House of Assembly which had but little sympathy with his views. That he did not accomplish more is less a matter of surprise than that he accomplished so much. With heavy odds against him, he contended for the rights of the people and the improvement of the constitution, and he lived to see the principles for which he had fought so firmly established in his native province that they can never be disturbed.

A CHAMPION OF THE PEOPLE

It was never his good fortune to be the leader and master of a government or to have a free hand in the work of legislation. We are therefore left in the dark as to what he might have accomplished under more favourable conditions. Yet there is but little doubt that, had he remained in public life, the progress of Reform would have been greatly accelerated, and that such important measures as the establishing of free schools would have been brought about much earlier than was the case without his vigorous support. The faults of Wilmot were those that belong to an ardent, enthusiastic and liberty-loving temperament. He hated injustice in every form, and in his denunciation of evil he was sometimes led to use stronger language than men of cooler feelings approved. In this way he aroused opposition and left himself open to attack. Yet it is doubtful whether the censure of his enemies was as injurious as the flattery of some who professed to be [139] his friends, and who were ready to applaud whatever he said or did. Being accepted as a leader when a mere youth because he had made a few eloquent speeches, he missed the wholesome discipline which most men have to undergo before they achieve fame. He would have been a greater and wiser man if he had been spared the unthinking flattery which was too lavishly bestowed upon him. Yet, after all has been said by those who would seek to minimize his merits, the fact remains that this son of New Brunswick stood for years as the foremost champion of the rights of the people, and that it is impossible to deny him a place among the great men who have assisted to build up Canada.

FOOTNOTES:

[9] The Aroostook War arose out of the unsettled boundary question between Maine and New Brunswick. There was a large area on

the St. John River, the ownership of which was in dispute, and in 1839 the difficulty came to a head in consequence of the governor of Maine undertaking to solve the question in his own way by taking possession of the territory. Governor Fairfield, of Maine, sent eighteen hundred militiamen to the front and Sir John Harvey, the governor of New Brunswick, issued a proclamation asserting the right of Great Britain to guard the territory while it was in dispute, and calling on the governor of Maine to withdraw his troops. Fairfield denied the right to issue a counter proclamation and called on the state for ten thousand men. Sir John Harvey then sent Colonel Maxwell with the 36th and 69th Regiments and a train of artillery to the upper St. John to watch the movements of the militia. A large force of New Brunswick militia was also embodied and sent to the front. Fortunately, President Van Buren sent General Winfield Scott to Maine with full power to settle the difficulty. He got into a friendly correspondence with Sir John Harvey, which led to an understanding by which the troops on both sides were withdrawn and all danger of war averted. The boundary question was afterwards settled by the Ashburton Treaty.

SIR LEONARD TILLEY

[143]

CHAPTER I
EARLY LIFE AND BUSINESS CAREER

The political career of Samuel Leonard Tilley did not begin until the year that brought the work of Lemuel Allan Wilmot as a legislator to a close. Both were elected members of the House of Assembly in 1850, but in the following year Wilmot was elevated to the bench, so that the province lost his services as a political reformer just as a new man, who was destined to win as great a reputation as himself, was stepping on the stage. Samuel Leonard Tilley was born at Gagetown, on the St. John River, on May 8th, 1818, just thirty-five years after the landing of his royalist grandfather at St. John. He passed away seventy-eight years later, full of years and honours, having won the highest prizes that it was in the power of his native province to bestow.

OF LOYALIST STOCK

In these days, when a man becomes eminent an effort is usually made to trace his descent from distinguished ancestors, but most of the early inhabitants of New Brunswick were too careless in such matters to leave much material to the modern maker of pedigrees. Sir Leonard Tilley was unable to trace his descent beyond his great-grandfather, Samuel Tilley. At one time it was thought that [144] his first ancestor in America was John Tilley, who came over in the *Mayflower* in 1620, but a closer search of the records of the Plymouth colony reveals the fact that John Tilley left no sons. But there were persons of the name of Tilley in the Massachusetts Bay colony as early as 1640, and there seems to be no doubt that Sir Leonard Tilley's ancestors had been long in America. They belonged to the respectable farming class which has given the Dominion of Canada and the United States so many of their most distinguished sons. Samuel Tilley, the great-grandfather of Sir Leonard, was a farmer on Long Island at the time of the American Revolution. His farm was then within the boundaries of the present borough of Brooklyn, and the curious in such matters can find the very lot upon which he resided laid down upon some of the ancient maps of that locality. At the time the British occupied Long Island, after the battle which took place there in the autumn of 1776, resulting in the defeat of the

Americans, the Brooklyn farmers were called upon to provide cattle for the sustenance of the troops. Samuel Tilley, being a loyal man and a friend of the government, complied, and for this he was made the subject of attacks by the disloyal element among his neighbours, and in the course of time was compelled to seek shelter within the British lines. The occupation of Long Island by the British during the whole period of the war made it secure enough for Samuel Tilley, as well [145] as for all loyal men who lived in the vicinity of Brooklyn; but when the war was over it became necessary for him to seek shelter in Nova Scotia, the acts of confiscation and banishment against the Loyalists being of the most severe character. Samuel Tilley came to New Brunswick with the spring fleet, which arrived in St. John in May, 1783, and was a grantee of Parrtown, which is now the city of St. John. He erected a house and store on King Street, on the south side, just to the east of Germain, and there commenced a business which he continued for several years. He died at St. John in the year 1815. His wife was Elizabeth Morgan, who survived him for many years and died in 1835, aged eighty-four years.

Sir Leonard Tilley was not born when his great-grandfather died, but had a clear recollection of his great-grandmother, who lived for about four years after he came to reside in St. John. James Tilley, the grandfather of Sir Leonard, was also a grantee of Parrtown, he having purchased for a trifling sum, when a boy, a lot on Princess Street, which had been drawn by some person who was anxious to dispose of it. James Tilley was a resident of Sunbury County and a magistrate there for a great many years, dying in the year 1851. Sir Leonard Tilley's father, Thomas Morgan Tilley, was born in 1790, and served his time with Israel Gove, who was a house-joiner and builder. He spent his early days as a lumberman, getting out ship timber, his operations [146] being carried on mainly at Tantiwanty, in the rear of Upper Gagetown. He afterwards went into business at Gagetown, and kept a store there down to the time of his death, which took place in 1870. Sir Leonard's great-grandmother, on his father's side, was Mary Chase, of the Chase family of Massachusetts, she having come from Freetown, in that state. Sir Leonard's mother was Susan Ann Peters, daughter of William Peters, who was for many years a prominent farmer in Queens County, and a member of the legislative assembly. William Peters owned a large property and had one of the finest tracts of land possessed by any man in the province in his day. But he was unwise enough to sell it for the purpose of obtaining money with which to enter into lumbering with William Wilmot, the father of L. A. Wilmot, and, being unsuccessful in his operations, his whole fortune was swept away. The ancestors of William Peters were from New York state, from which they came with the rest of the Loyalists in 1783.

EARLY EDUCATION

The house in Gagetown in which the future governor of New Brunswick and finance minister of Canada was born, is still standing and is now used as a hotel. Gagetown was at that period, and still is, one of the most beautiful places in New Brunswick. The river St. John flows in front of it, and Gagetown Creek, which is almost as wide as the river, laves its shores. The land in the vicinity is fertile, and fine old trees line the streets, giving [147] an air of beauty and refinement to the locality. Sir Leonard was named after his uncle, Samuel Leonard Peters, and the latter was named after an English schoolmaster named Samuel Leonard, who was a great favourite with William Peters, the grandfather of the subject of this biography. Samuel Leonard, after leaving Gagetown, appears to have removed to Nova Scotia, and probably died in that province. When Sir Leonard was five years old he was sent to the Madras School in Gagetown, of which Samuel Babbitt was the teacher. He attended this school from 1823 until 1827, when the grammar school was instituted in Gagetown. The Madras school system was at that time in high favour with the people of the province, and these schools received large grants from the government, it being thought that this system was more advantageous than any other for the instruction of youth. This idea, however, did not prove to be universally correct, for in the course of a few years we find the legislature declaring that while they believed the Madras system suitable to towns and populous places, it did not answer so well in rural districts. Samuel Babbitt, the teacher of the Madras School, was clerk of the parish, and, according to the custom of that day, led the responses in church. The rector of Gagetown at this period was the Rev. Samuel Clark. The teacher of the local grammar school which young Tilley attended from 1827 to 1831 was William Jenkins, a graduate of [148] Dublin University. Jenkins was a very severe man, and believed in the doctrine that he who spares the rod spoils the child, and Sir Leonard had a very vivid recollection of the vigour with which he applied the birch. He removed from Gagetown shortly after 1831, and took up his residence in Quebec, where he conducted a large school for many years, dying about the year 1863. Sir Leonard, after he had become a well-known political character and a member of the government of New Brunswick, had the pleasure of paying him a visit some time in 1858.

An interesting incident occurred in 1827, at the time young Tilley commenced to attend the grammar school. Sir Howard Douglas, who was then governor of New Brunswick, paid a visit to Gagetown and was the guest of Colonel Harry Peters, the speaker of the House of Assembly. While the governor and his host were walking through Gagetown, they met young Tilley and a son of Harry Peters returning from school, and the boys were introduced to His Excellency, who presented each of them with a Spanish quarter-dollar. Sir Leonard could remember and often spoke of the appearance of Sir Howard Douglas, dressed in a blue coat with brass buttons, a fine-looking gentleman, with a pleasant face and a kindly smile. Little thought the then governor of New Brunswick that the boy to whom he was speaking, a lad of nine years of age, would fifty years [149] later sit in his own chair in the government house.

ENTERS ON BUSINESS LIFE

Young Tilley was not the kind of youth likely to be satisfied to reside all his life in Gagetown. Other boys of less ambition might be content to settle down on the farm and to fulfil their destinies within the comparatively limited sphere of action which that little town in Queens County afforded, but he had within him longings for a higher destiny than he was likely to attain as a resident of a rural district.

Young Tilley came to St. John in May, 1831, at the age of thirteen. He at once entered the drugstore of Dr. Henry Cook, as a clerk, it being the fashion of those times for medical men to have a dispensary in connection with their professional practice, so that they could give advice, and dispense their own prescriptions with equal facility. He continued as clerk with Dr. Cook until February, 1835, when he entered the service of William O. Smith, who, in later years, was mayor of St. John. It was while a clerk with Smith that Tilley became a member of the St. John Young Men's Debating Society, an organization which, if it has no other claim to the remembrance of posterity, at least has that of giving one distinguished statesman to British America, and a governor to New Brunswick. It was in this society that he made his first attempt at public speaking, and it may be said that from the very beginning he showed [150] a remarkable aptitude for debate and public discussions.

In December, 1837, he took one of the most important steps of his life in espousing the cause of total abstinence. Having taken up this movement, he threw his whole energy into it, and from that time down to the day of his death he was a consistent temperance man, and a strong advocate of the principle of total abstinence. It was, perhaps, this strong advocacy of the cause of temperance, more than anything else, that brought him before the public as a suitable person to become a candidate for the House of Assembly, and led to his first election as a representative for the city of St. John in the local legislature thirteen years later. Certainly the fact that Tilley, from that time until the close of his public career, had always the support of the temperance societies, gave him a strength which he hardly would have obtained otherwise, and rallied around him a phalanx of friends, who, for fidelity to his interests and zeal for his political advancement, could hardly have been surpassed.

Tilley commenced business on his own account in 1838, before he had attained the age of twenty years, as a member of the firm of Peters & Tilley, and he continued a successful career until 1855, when he transferred his business to Mr. T. B. Barker, the founder of the present firm of T. B. Barker & Sons. It is unnecessary to say anything more in regard to Mr. Tilley's life as a business man [151] than that it was a highly prosperous one. He showed so much energy and enterprise that when he entered political life he was comparatively wealthy. There is no doubt that if he had continued in business instead of devoting his energies to the service of the province and Dominion, he would have made far more money than he obtained as a politician.

COLONIAL TRADE

The movement in behalf of free trade, which was changing the fiscal policy of the United Kingdom in the closing years of the first half of the nineteenth century, did not meet with much favour in New Brunswick, because it seriously affected the leading industry of the province. Colonial timber had long enjoyed a preference in the British market, but this preference had been seriously impaired by imperial legislation and was likely to be taken away altogether if free trade principles should prevail. Many remonstrances had been sent to the British government against the reduction or abolition of the duty on foreign timber which came into competition with the colonial product, but these remonstrances proved wholly unavailing, and it was seriously believed that the colonial timber trade would be destroyed. This led to the annexation movement of 1848, which affected all the provinces, while it also caused the formation of organizations pledged to resist the free trade movement. Tilley was in sympathy with these efforts to preserve colonial trade, and it was in consequence [152] of this that he first made his entrance into political life.

GENERAL ELECTION OF 1850

At a meeting of the electors of St. John in favour of protection, which was held previous to the general election of 1850, Tilley was nominated as one of the candidates for the city of St. John. He was not present at the meeting and had no knowledge whatever of the intention of the electors to make such a nomination. A meeting was called a few nights later in Carleton to confirm the nomination, and at that meeting Tilley was present. He then made the strongest possible protest against the nomination, but the electors present would not take "No" for an answer, and he eventually consented to stand as a candidate, informing them at the same time that he had an engagement to be in Boston on the day fixed for the nomination, and could not be at the hustings on that day. Notwithstanding this statement they still persisted in his nomination, but as Tilley was absent in the United States, his nomination speech on that occasion was made by Joseph W. Lawrence, who afterwards was found among his strongest political opponents. At the general election of 1850 all the candidates elected for the city and county of St. John were avowed opponents of the government. Tilley was returned at the head of the poll, while W. H. Needham, who ran with him, was likewise elected. The members elected for the county were R. D. Wilmot, William J. Ritchie, John H. Gray and Charles Simonds; [153] while J. R. Partelow, Charles Watters and John Jordan were the three defeated candidates. The list of candidates for the city and county of St. John included two future governors, a future chief-justice of the supreme court of Canada and two other judges, to say nothing of the provincial secretary, Mr. Partelow, a speaker of the House of Assembly and a future mayor of St. John. It must be admitted that few elections that have ever been held in any part of British North America have had so many candidates presented to the electors who were afterwards eminent in public life. This election took place at an important epoch in the history of the province, when the old order was passing away and men's minds were prepared for a great change in political affairs. It was a Reform House of Assembly, and, although all the members elected for the purpose of upholding Reform principles did not prove true to their trust, still it contained a larger number of men of Liberal views than any of its predecessors.

Among the members of this House were several who had taken a very important part in public affairs, or who afterwards became members of the executive. The county of York sent among its representatives, Lemuel A. Wilmot, who had been a member of the House for sixteen years, and who had taken a leading part in many measures of importance for the improvement of the system by which the country was governed. [154]

Mr. Charles Fisher, who had been a colleague of Mr. Wilmot in the county of York, was defeated at the general election, but soon afterwards became a member of the House. Mr. Fisher had not the oratorical gifts possessed by Mr. Wilmot, but he was even stronger in his Liberal views, and as a constitutional lawyer he had no equal, at that time, in the province. Although his manners were somewhat uncouth and his address far from polished, Fisher had strong individuality and a singularly clear intellect. His services in the cause of Liberalism in New Brunswick can hardly be overestimated, and these services were rendered at a time when to be a Liberal was to be, to a large extent, ostracized by the great and powerful who looked upon any interference with their vested rights as little short of treason.

Tilley's colleague from St. John city was William H. Needham, who afterwards represented the county of York in the legislature. Mr. Needham had some remarkable gifts as a speaker and a public man, and he might have risen to a much higher position than he ever attained had it not been that his principles were somewhat uncertain. In truth, Needham never succeeded in getting sufficiently clear of the world to be quite independent, and this misfortune hampered him greatly in his political career.

NOTABLE CANDIDATES

One of the members from St. John County was William J. Ritchie, a lawyer who had risen by his own efforts to a commanding position at the bar, [155] and who became chief-justice of Canada. Mr. Ritchie had been a member of the House of Assembly for several years, and always a useful one. He possessed what few members at that time had, — a clear knowledge of the true principles of responsible government. He had an eminently practical mind; he was a forcible and impressive speaker, and he was bold in the enunciation of the Liberal principles to which he held. It was a serious misfortune to the province that at a comparatively early age he was transferred to the bench, so that his great abilities were lost at a critical period when they might have been useful to New Brunswick in many ways.

John H. Gray, a new member, also sat in this House for the county of St. John. Mr. Gray was a man of fine presence, handsome appearance, and had a style of oratory that was very captivating and impressive. His fluency, however, was greater than his ability, and he injured himself by deserting the Liberal party, which he had been elected to uphold. Gray never quite recovered from the unpopularity connected with this action, and he never became in any sense a real leader. The party he had deserted soon obtained the control of the province, and his final appearance in the legislature was as a supporter of Mr. Tilley, content to play a secondary part during the great confederation conflict.

Robert Duncan Wilmot, another of the St. John [156] County members, a first cousin of L. A. Wilmot, was not new to the legislature, and his mind being naturally conservative, it is in connection with the Conservative party that he is best known in the history of the province. He was elected as a Liberal, however, in 1850, but seems to have forgotten that fact as soon as he reached the House of Assembly. This was not the only occasion on which Wilmot contrived to change his principles, for he performed a similar feat during the confederation contest, and left the anti-confederate government of 1865 in the lurch at a moment when its existence almost depended on his fidelity. Wilmot never was an eloquent man, and he entertained some highly visionary views in regard to an irredeemable paper currency, but he was a useful public servant, and he afterwards became a member of the government of Canada and eventually lieutenant-governor of New Brunswick.

JOHN R. PARTELOW

The Hon. John R. Partelow, who was defeated in St. John but elected for Victoria, was a man who might have acquired a great political reputation had the stage on which he appeared been a larger one. Partelow's qualifications for high public position did not depend upon his oratory, which was not of a high order, but upon his moderation and good sense. Partelow's origin was humble, and his early days were spent as a clerk in a store on the North Wharf, St. John. In that subordinate position he made himself so useful and displayed [157] so much ability that he was marked for promotion. The idea of bringing him forward as a candidate for the city of St. John seems to have originated with his employers, but when he gained a seat in the legislature he speedily made his influence felt. Partelow spoke but seldom, but when he did address the legislature it was generally with good effect, and after the subject had been to a large extent exhausted by previous speakers. He then had a faculty of drafting a resolution which seemed to express the general sense of all, and which was usually accepted as a solution of the matter. He was a good business man, understood accounts thoroughly and, therefore, had a great advantage in legislative work over those who were not so well equipped in this respect. New Brunswick may have produced greater men than he in public life, but none whose talents were more useful to the province, or better fitted to serve its interests at a critical period in its constitutional history.

[159]

CHAPTER II
ELECTED TO THE LEGISLATURE

Shortly after the general election, Chief-Justice Chipman, who had been in infirm health, resigned his office, and a vacancy was thus left on the bench of the supreme court of the province. In the natural course, this office ought to have gone to the attorney-general, Mr. L. A. Wilmot, but this appointment was not made. The council were unable to unite in any recommendation to the governor, who consequently laid all the facts before the home government and in reply received instructions to give the chief-justiceship to Judge Carter and to offer the puisne judgeship to Mr. Wilmot, or, if he should refuse it, to Mr. Kinnear, the solicitor-general. The executive council complained that the appointment of Mr. Wilmot to a seat on the bench by the authority of the secretary of state without the advice or recommendation of the responsible executive within the province, was at variance with the principles of responsible government which were understood to be in force. They, however, had only themselves to thank for this, for they were continually appealing to Downing Street. As a majority of the House had been elected as opponents of the government, it was supposed there [160] would be no difficulty in bringing about a change of administration. Mr. Simonds, of St. John, who was reputed to be a Liberal, was elected speaker without opposition, and at an early day in the session Mr. Ritchie, of St. John, moved, as an amendment to the address, a want-of-confidence resolution. This resolution, instead of being carried by a large majority as was expected, was lost by a vote of fifteen to twenty-two, Messrs. Alexander Rankine and John T. Williston, of Northumberland, Messrs. Robert Gordon and Joseph Reed, of Gloucester, Mr. A. Barbarie, of Restigouche, and Mr. Francis McPhelim, of Kent, having deserted their Liberal allies. Had they proved faithful, the government would have been defeated, and the province would have been spared another three years of an incompetent administration.

In this division, Tilley and Needham, who represented the city of St. John, and Messrs. R. D. Wilmot and Gray, two of the county members, voted for Ritchie's amendment. As Wilmot and Gray showed by their votes that they had no confidence in the government in February, 1851, it was with much surprise that the people of St. John, in the August following, learned that they had become members of the administration which they had so warmly condemned a few months before. Their secession from the Liberal party destroyed whatever chance had before existed of ousting the government. Mr. Fisher had seceded from the government [161] in consequence of their action in reference to the judicial appointments, and John Ambrose Street, who was a member for Northumberland, became attorney-general in place of Robert Parker, appointed a judge. Mr. Street was a ready debater and a strong Conservative, and his entrance into the government at that time showed that a Conservative policy was to be maintained.

RAILWAY LEGISLATION

Mr. Street, as leader of the government in the assembly, presented a long programme of measures for the consideration of the legislature, none of which proved to be of any particular value. The municipal corporation bill was passed, but it was a permissive measure, and was not taken advantage of by any of the counties. A bill to make the legislative council elective, which was also passed in the Lower House at the instance of the government, was defeated in the Upper Chamber. The bill appointing commissioners on law reform was carried, and resulted in the production of the three volumes of the revised statutes issued in 1854. The most important bill of the session, introduced by the government, was one in aid of the construction of a railroad from St. John to Shediac. This bill provided that the government should give a company two hundred and fifty thousand pounds sterling, to assist in the construction of the line referred to. There was also a bill to assist the St. Andrews and Quebec Railroad to the extent of fifty thousand pounds, and a bonus or subvention to [162] the Shediac line amounting to upwards of eleven thousand dollars a mile, for which sum a very good railway could be constructed at the present time. It may be stated here that, although the company was formed and undertook to build a railway to Shediac under the terms offered by the government, the province had eventually to build the road at a cost of forty thousand dollars a mile, or fully double what a similar road could be constructed for now.

KING'S COLLEGE

One of the measures brought forward by the government at this session was with reference to the schools of the province. The idea of taxing the property of the county for the support of public schools had not then found any general acceptance in New Brunswick; indeed, it was not till the year 1872 that the measure embodying this principle was passed by the legislature. The government school bill of 1851 provided that the teachers were to be paid in money, or board and lodging, by the district to the amount of ten pounds for six months, in addition to the government allowance. This bill was a very slight improvement on the Act then in force, and as the government left it to the House to deal with, and did not press it as a government measure, it was not passed. A private member, Mr. Gilbert, of Queens, at this session proposed to convert King's College into an agricultural school, with a model farm attached. King's College had been established by an Act [163] passed in 1829, and had received a large endowment from the province, but it never was a popular institution because of its connection with a single Church. The original charter of the college made the bishop of the diocese the visitor, and required the president to be always a clergyman of the Church of England; and, although this had been changed in 1845 by the legislature, the number of students who attended it was always small, and it was shown in the course of debate that it had failed to fulfil the object for which it was created. The college council consisted of fifteen members, of whom ten were Episcopalians; and the visitor, the chancellor, the president, the principal, five out of seven of the professors and teachers, and the two examiners were members of the same Church. The services in the college chapel were required to be attended by all resident students, and of the eighteen students then in the college, sixteen were Episcopalians. It was felt that this college required to be placed on a different footing, and Mr. Gilbert's bill, although it provoked much hostile comment at the time, certainly would have been more beneficial to the educational interests of the country, if it had passed, than the state of affairs which resulted from the continuance of the old system. An agricultural school was the very thing the province required, while, judging from the limited attendance at the college at that time, the people of this province were not greatly impressed

[164] with the value of a classical education. In 1851, however, any one who proposed to replace a college for the teaching of Greek and Latin with a college of agriculture, and the sciences allied to it, was looked upon as a Philistine. Then youths were taught to compose Latin and to read Greek who never, to the day of their death, had a competent knowledge of their own language; and agricultural studies, which were of the highest importance to more than one-half of the people of the province, were totally neglected. Mr. Gilbert's bill was defeated, as it was certain to be in a legislature which was still under the domination of old ideas. Had it passed, New Brunswick might at this time have had a large body of scientific farmers capable of cultivating the soil in the most efficient manner, and increasing its productiveness to an extent hardly dreamed of by those who only consider it in the light of the present system of cultivation.

During this session, Mr. Ritchie of St. John moved a series of resolutions condemning the government, and complaining of the colonial office and of the conduct of the governor. These resolutions declared: first, that the House was entitled to full copies of all despatches addressed to or received from the colonial office, and that it was not enough merely to send extracts from a despatch which had been received by the governor. They declared that the power of making appointments to offices was [165] vested in the governor by and with the advice of the executive council, and that the appointment of the chief-justice and a puisne judge by the governor, contrary to the advice of his council, was inconsistent with the principles of responsible government. They complained that the salaries were excessive, and condemned the refusal of the British government to allow the colonies to grant bounties for the development of their resources. These resolutions, after being debated for about a week, were rejected by a vote of twenty-one to nineteen, the smallness of the majority against them at the time being looked upon as virtually a Liberal victory. If the nineteen had been made up of men who could be relied on to stand by their colours in all emergencies, it would have been a Liberal triumph, but, unfortunately, among the nineteen there were some who afterwards deserted their party for the sake of offices and power.

A POLITICAL SURPRISE

Early in August it was announced that John H. Gray and R. D. Wilmot, two of the Liberal members for the county of St. John, had abandoned their party and their principles and become members of the government. The Liberals of St. John, who had elected these gentlemen by a substantial majority, were naturally chagrined at such a proof of their faithlessness, and their colleagues were likewise greatly annoyed. Messrs. Gray and Wilmot made the usual excuses of all deserters for their conduct, the principal one being that they thought [166] they could serve the interests of the constituency and of the province better by being in the government than out of it. The friends of the four members who still remained faithful, Messrs. Tilley, Simonds, Ritchie and Needham, held a meeting at which these gentlemen were present, and it was agreed that they should join in an address to their constituents condemning the course of Messrs. Wilmot and Gray, and calling on the constituency to pronounce judgment upon it. As Wilmot, who had been appointed to the office of surveyor-general, had to return to his constituency for reëlection, the voice of the constituency could only be ascertained by placing a candidate in the field in opposition to him. This was done, and Mr. Allan McLean was elected to oppose Mr. Wilmot. The result seemed to show that the people of St. John had condoned the offence, for Wilmot was reëlected by a majority of two hundred and seventy-three. As this appeared to be a proof that they had lost the confidence of their constituents, Messrs. Simonds, Ritchie and Tilley at once resigned their seats and did not offer for reëlection. This act was, at the time, thought by many to indicate an excess of sensitiveness, and Needham refused to follow their example, thereby forfeiting the regard of most of those who had formerly supported him. The sequel proved that the three resigning members were right, for they won much more in public respect by their conduct than they [167] lost by their temporary exclusion from the House of Assembly.

THE ST. JOHN ELECTION

The gentlemen returned for the three seats in St. John which had been vacated by the resigning members were James A. Harding, John Goddard and John Johnson. Mr. Harding, who ran for the city, was opposed by S. K. Foster. Harding was a Liberal, but this fact does not seem to have been kept in view when he was elected. The net result of the whole affair was that the constituency of St. John could not be relied upon to support a Liberal principle, or any kind of principle as against men. That has always been a peculiarity of the St. John constituencies, men being more important than measures, and frequently a mere transient feeling being set off against the most important considerations of general policy.

Tilley was not in the House of Assembly during the sessions of 1852, 1853 and 1854; that period was one, however, of development in political matters and of substantial progress. The governor's speech at the opening of the session of 1852 was largely devoted to railways, and it expressed the opinion that a railroad connecting Canada and Nova Scotia, and a connection with a line from St. John to the United States, would produce an abundant return to the province, and that by this means millions of tons of timber, then standing worthless in the forest, would find a profitable market. It was during this session that Messrs. Peto, Brassy [168] and Betts proposed to construct the European and North American Railway, on certain conditions. The subsidies offered by the province at this time were twenty thousand pounds a year for twenty years, and a million acres of land for the European and North American Railway, as the line to the United States was termed; and for the Quebec line, twenty-two thousand pounds sterling for twenty years, and two million acres of land. A new company, which included Mr. Jackson, M. P., offered to build the New Brunswick section of both railroads, upon the province granting them a subsidy of twenty thousand pounds a year for twenty years, and four million acres of land. Attorney-General Street introduced a series of railway resolutions favouring the building of the Intercolonial Railway jointly by the three provinces, according to terms which had been agreed upon by the delegates of each. The arrangement was that the Intercolonial Railway should be built through the valley of the St. John, and for favouring resolutions in the House confirming this arrangement, Mr. Street's Northumberland constituents called upon him to resign his seat, a step which he refused to take.

INTERCOLONIAL RAILWAY

The government railway resolutions were carried by a large majority. During the recess Mr. Chandler, as a representative of New

Brunswick, and Mr. Hincks, a representative of Canada, went to London to endeavour to obtain from the British government a sum sufficient to build the Intercolonial [169] Railway. The request of the delegates was refused on the ground that such a work had to be one of military necessity, and that the route which had been selected, by the valley of the St. John, was not a proper one for military purposes. As Mr. Chandler could not obtain what he wished from the British government, he applied to Messrs. Peto, Brassy and Betts, who said they were prepared to build all the railroads that New Brunswick might require, upon the most advantageous terms. Mr. Jackson visited the province in September of the same year, and it was agreed that his company should build a railway from St. John to Amherst, and from St. John to the United States frontier, the distance being then estimated at two hundred and fourteen miles, for the sum of sixty-five hundred pounds sterling per mile. The province was to take stock to the extent of twelve hundred pounds per mile, and to lend its bonds to the company for one thousand eight hundred pounds additional per mile. The completion of this arrangement caused great rejoicing in the province, especially in St. John, a special session of the legislature being called on October 21st for the express purpose of amending the Railway Act so that it might conform to the new conditions. As both branches of the legislature were strongly in favour of the railway policy of the government, the necessary bills were speedily passed and the legislature was prorogued after a session of eight days. [170]

The meeting of the legislature in 1853 derived its principal importance from the fact that much of its time was taken up with the discussion of the question of a reciprocity treaty with the United States of America. The discussion disclosed a strong disinclination on the part of many members to any arrangement by which the fisheries would be surrendered. An address to the queen was agreed to by both branches of the legislature in which it was stated that the exclusive use of the fisheries by the inhabitants of British North America would be much more advantageous and satisfactory than anything which the United States could offer as an equivalent. It was also stated that no reciprocity treaty with that country would be satisfactory to New Brunswick which did not embrace the free exchange of raw materials and natural products and the admission of colonial built vessels to registry in American ports. The tone of the discussions on this subject, both in 1853 and 1854, shows that reciprocity with the United States was not generally regarded as being an equivalent for the giving of the fisheries to our neighbours, and it is quite clear that, so far as New Brunswick was concerned, the reciprocity treaty would not have been agreed to had it not been that the matter was in the hands of the British government, and that the legislature of the province was not disposed to resist strenuously any arrangement which that government thought it wise to make.

[171]

CHAPTER III
THE PROHIBITORY LIQUOR LAW

The House which had been elected in 1850 was dissolved after the prorogation in 1854, and the election came on in the month of July. It was a memorable occasion, because it was certain that the topics discussed by the House then to be elected would be of the very highest importance. One of these subjects was the reciprocity treaty, which at that time had been arranged with the United States through the British government. This treaty provided for the free interchange of certain natural products between the great republic and the several provinces which later formed the Dominion of Canada, and it had been brought about through the efforts of Lord Elgin, who at that time was governor-general of Canada. The treaty was agreed to on June 5th, and was subject to ratification by the imperial parliament and the legislatures of the British North American colonies which were affected by it. In the St. John constituencies there was at that time a strong feeling in favour of a protection policy, but this did not interfere with the desire to effect the interchange of raw material with the United States on advantageous terms. Tilley had been originally [172] nominated as a protectionist, and still held views favourable to the encouragement and protection of native industries by means of the tariff, but he was also favourable to reciprocity with the United States if it could be obtained in such a manner as to be beneficial to the province. At the general election he led the poll in the city of St. John, his colleague being James A. Harding, who had been elected at a bye-election to the previous House. For the county, Mr. William J. Ritchie was one of the successful candidates, and the only Liberal returned for that constituency. The other members for the county were the Hon. John R. Partelow, Robert D. Wilmot and John H. Gray.

The new House was called together on October 19th for the purpose of ratifying the reciprocity treaty, and the Hon. D. L. Hanington was elected speaker by a vote of twenty-three to thirteen. This gave the opposition an earlier opportunity of defeating the Street-Partelow administration than would, under ordinary circumstances, have been possible. An amendment to the address was moved by the Hon. Charles Fisher, which was an indictment of the government for their various shortcomings and offences. The amendment was to expunge the whole of the fifth paragraph and substitute for it the following: —

"It is with feelings of loyalty and attachment to Her Majesty's person and government that we recognize, in that provision of the treaty which [173] requires the concurrence of this legislature, a distinct avowal by the imperial government of their determination to preserve inviolate the principles of self-government, and to regard the constitution of the province as sacred as that of the parent state. We regret that the conduct of the administration during the last few years has not been in accordance with these principles, and we feel constrained thus early to state to your Excellency that your constitutional advisers have not conducted the government of the province in the true spirit of our colonial constitution." This amendment was debated for six days, and was carried by a vote of twenty-seven to twelve.

QUESTION OF THE JUDGES REVIVED

The general ground of accusation against the government, and the one most strongly insisted upon, was that it had yielded to the influence of the colonial office in the appointment of Judge Wilmot. It was well known that the government at that time, or at least a majority of them, did not consider it necessary to appoint another judge; at all events, they took no steps to bring about another appointment; but they yielded to the colonial office, and the pressure put upon them by Sir Edmund Head, the lieutenant-governor, so far as to acquiesce in the appointment of Judge Carter as chief-justice, and the elevation of Mr. Wilmot to the bench. This was a fair ground of attack, because it was clear that if the executive council of New Brunswick was under the orders of the home government, [174] representative institutions and responsible government did not exist.

Thus the Street-Partelow government fell, and with it disappeared, at once and forever, the old Conservative régime which had existed in the province from its foundation, and which, unavoidably no doubt, had presided over the early political life of the colony, but the undue continuance of which was wholly incompatible with the full development of representative institutions and responsible government. It was a great triumph for the cause of Liberalism that the Conservatives of that period were not only defeated, but swept altogether out of existence. After that a government of men who called themselves Conservatives might go into power, but the old state of affairs, under which the lieutenant-governor could exercise almost despotic powers, had departed forever, and could no more be revived than the heptarchy. All that a Conservative government could do after that was to fall into line with the policy of the men they had displaced, and proceed, less rapidly perhaps, but none the less surely, along the path of political progress.

The new government which was formed as the result of this vote had for its premier the Hon. Charles Fisher, who took the office of attorney-general; Mr. Tilley became provincial secretary; Mr. James Brown, a few weeks later, received the office of surveyor-general; J. M. Johnson, one of the members for Northumberland, became solicitor-general; [175] and William J. Ritchie, Albert J. Smith and William H. Steeves were members of the government without office.

The bill to give effect to the reciprocity treaty passed its third reading on November 2d, only five members voting against it. On motion of the Hon. Mr. Ritchie, one of the members of the new government, it was resolved that it was desirable and expedient that the surveyor-general, who was a political officer, should hold a seat in the House of Assembly, and that the government should carry out the wishes of the House in this respect. Before the House again met the wishes of the House had been complied with, and Mr. Brown, of Charlotte, became surveyor-general.

SESSION OF 1855

The House met again on February 1st, 1855, and then the real work of legislative and administrative reform began. In the speech from the throne it was stated that the Customs Act would expire in the course of a year, and that it was necessary that a new Act should be passed. A better system of auditing the public accounts was also recommended, and a better system of electing members to the legislature. On March 5th, correspondence was brought down, dated the previous 15th of August, announcing, on the part of the imperial government, the withdrawal of the imperial customs establishment, which was considered to be no longer necessary, and stating that as the duties of these offices were now mainly in connection with [176] the registration of vessels in the colonies, and the granting of certificates of the origin of colonial products, this work would hereafter be performed by the colonial officers. A letter addressed to the comptrollers and other customs officers had informed them that their services would be discontinued after January 5th, 1855. So disappeared the last remnant of the old imperial custom-house system, which had been the cause of so many difficulties in all the colonies and which had done more than anything else to bring about the revolution which separated the thirteen colonies from the mother country.

The great measure of the session of 1855 was the law to prevent the importation, manufacture or selling of liquor. This bill was brought in by Mr. Tilley as a private member, and not on behalf of the government. It was introduced on March 3d. Considering its importance and the fact that it led to a crisis in the affairs of the government and the temporary defeat of the Liberal party, it went through the House with comparatively little difficulty. It was first considered on March 19th, and a motion to postpone its further consideration for three months was lost by a vote of seventeen to twenty-one. The final division on the third reading was taken on March 27th, and the vote was twenty-one to eighteen, so that every member of the House, with one exception, voted yea or nay. The closeness of this last division should have warned [177] the advocate of the measure that it was likely to produce difficulty, for it is clear that all laws which are intended to regulate the personal habits of men must be ineffectual unless they have the support of a large majority of the people affected by them. That this was not the case with the prohibitory liquor law was shown by the vote in the legislature, and it was still more clearly shown after the law came into operation on January 1st, 1856.

PROHIBITORY LIQUOR ACT

The passage of the prohibitory law was a bold experiment, and, as the sequel showed, more bold than wise. The temperance movement in New Brunswick, at that time, was hardly more than twenty years old, and New Brunswick had always been a province in which the consumption of liquor was large in proportion to its population. When it was first settled by the Loyalists, and for many years afterwards, the use of liquor was considered necessary to happiness, if not to actual existence. Every person consumed spirits, which generally came to the province in the form of Jamaica rum, from the West Indies, and as this rum was supposed to be an infallible cure for nearly every ill that flesh is heir to, nothing could be done at that time without its use. Large quantities of rum were taken into the woods for the lumbermen, to give them sufficient strength to perform the laborious work in which they were engaged, and if it had been suggested that a time would come when the same work would be done without any more powerful [178] stimulant than tea, the person who ventured to make such a suggestion would have been regarded as foolish. Experience has shown that more and better work can be done, not only in the woods, but everywhere else, without the use of stimulants than with them; but no one could be persuaded to believe this sixty years ago. Every kind of work connected with the farm then had to be performed by the aid of liquor. Every house-raising, every ploughing match, every meeting at which farmers congregated, had unlimited quantities of rum as one of its leading features. It was also used by almost every man as a part of his regular diet; the old stagers had their eleven-o'clock dram and their nip before dinner; their regular series of drinks in the afternoon and evening; and they actually believed that without them life would not be worth living. Some idea of the extent of the spirit-drinking of the province may be gathered from the fact that, in 1838, when the population did not exceed 120,000, 312,298 gallons of rum, gin and whiskey, and 64,579 gallons of brandy were consumed in New Brunswick. Spirits, especially rum, were very cheap, and, the duty being only thirty cents a gallon, every one could afford to drink it if disposed to do so.

It was at midnight on December 31st, 1855, when the bells rang out a merry peal to announce the advent of the New Year, that this law went into force. This meant little less than a revolution in [179] the views, feelings and ideas of the people of the province, and, to a large extent, in their business relations. The liquor trade, both wholesale and retail, employed large numbers of men, and occupied many buildings which brought in large rents to their owners. The number of taverns in St. John and its suburb, Portland, was not less than two hundred, and every one of these establishments had to be closed. There were probably at least twenty men who sold liquor at wholesale, and who extended their business to every section of the province, as well as to parts of Nova Scotia, and their operations also had to come to an end. It was not to be supposed that these people would consent to be deprived suddenly of their means of living, especially in view of the fact that it was by no means certain that the sentiment in favour of prohibition was as strong in the country as it appeared to be in the legislature. It has always been understood that many men voted for prohibition in the House of Assembly who themselves were not total abstainers, but who thought they might make political capital by taking that course, and who relied on the legislative council to throw out the bill. No men were more disgusted and disappointed than they when the council passed the bill.

PROHIBITORY ACT UNPOPULAR

The result of the attempt to enforce prohibition was what might have been expected. The law was resisted, liquor continued to be sold, and when attempts were made to prevent the violation of the [180] law, and the violators of the law were brought before the courts, able lawyers were employed to defend them, while the sale of liquor by the same parties was continued, thus setting the law at defiance. This state of confusion lasted for several months, but it is unnecessary to go into details. In the city of St. John, especially, the conflict became bitter to the last degree, and it was evident that, however admirable prohibition might be of itself, the people of that city were not then prepared to accept it. At this juncture came the astounding news that the lieutenant-governor, the Hon. H. T. Manners-Sutton, had dissolved the House of Assembly against the advice of his council. This governor, who had been appointed the year previous, was a member of an old Conservative family, one of whom was speaker of the British House of Commons for a great many years. The traditions of this family were all opposed to such a radical measure as the prohibitory law, and, therefore, it was not to be expected that Manners-Sutton, who drank wine at his own table, and who considered that its use was proper and necessary, would be favourable to the law. But even if he had been disposed to favour it originally, or to regard it without prejudice, the confusion which it caused in the province when the attempt was made to enforce it, would naturally incline him to look upon it as an evil. At all events, he came to the conclusion that the people should have another opportunity of pronouncing [181] upon it, and, as the result of this view of the situation, resolved to dissolve the legislature, which had been elected only a little more than a year, and had still three years to run.

DISSOLUTION OF LEGISLATURE

The election which followed in July, 1856, was perhaps the most hotly contested that has ever taken place in the province. In St. John, especially, the conflict was fierce and bitter, because it was in this city that the liquor interest was strongest and most influential. All over the province, however, the people became interested in the struggle, as they had not been in any previous campaign.

By the Liberals and friends of the government, the action of Governor Sutton was denounced as tyrannical, unjust and entirely contrary to the principles of responsible government. On the other hand, the friends of the governor and of the liquor interest declared that his action was right, and the cry of "Support the governor," was raised in every county. At this day it is easy enough to discern that there was a good deal of unnecessary violence injected into the campaign, and that neither party was inclined to do full justice to the other.

[183]

CHAPTER IV
REFORM AND PROGRESS

The result of the election was the defeat of the government. Mr. Tilley lost his seat for St. John city, and the Hon. James Brown, the surveyor-general, was rejected by the county of Charlotte, so that two of the principal members of the executive were not in their places when the House was called together in July. The city of St. John, and the city and county of St. John, sent a solid phalanx of six members opposed to prohibition, and an Act repealing the prohibitory liquor law was passed by a vote of thirty-eight to two. The new government which was formed had for its principal members, the Hon. John H. Gray, who became attorney-general; the Hon. John C. Allen, solicitor-general; the Hon. R. D. Wilmot, provincial secretary; the Hon. John Montgomery, surveyor-general, and the Hon. Francis McPhelim, postmaster-general. The other members of the executive council were the Hon. Edward B. Chandler, the Hon. Robert L. Hazen and the Hon. Charles McPherson.

When the House met in July, the Hon. Charles Simonds, of St. John, was elected speaker, and it was soon discovered, after the liquor bill had been [184] disposed of, that the majority supporting the government was so small as to make it impossible for them to accomplish any useful legislation. When the legislature again met, in the early part of 1857, it was seen that in a House of forty-one members twenty were arrayed against the government, and the only way in which government business could be done was by the casting vote of the speaker. This condition of affairs speedily became intolerable, because it practically made legislation impossible, but it was brought to an end by Mr. McMonagle, one of the members for the county of Kings, withdrawing his support from the government. Two courses only were now open to them, to tender their resignations or advise the dissolution of the legislature, and they chose the latter. The House of Assembly was dissolved by proclamation on April 1st, 1857, and the writs for the election were made returnable on May 16th.

THE FISHER GOVERNMENT

The excitement attending this second election was, if possible, even greater than during the election of 1856, for the public mind had been wrought up to a high state of tension by the proceedings in the House and the numerous divisions in which the government was supported only by the casting vote of the speaker. The result of the election was so unfavourable to the Gray-Wilmot government that they at once tendered their resignations to the lieutenant-governor, agreeing to hold office only until their successors were appointed. [185] The most bitter contest of the election centred in the city of St. John, and it resulted in the election of Mr. Tilley, with Mr. James A. Harding for his colleague, the latter having changed his views in regard to the question at issue since the previous election, when he was chosen as an opponent of the government of which Tilley had been a member. When the Gray-Wilmot government resigned, the lieutenant-governor sent for Mr. Fisher, and entrusted to him the business of forming a new government. The government thus formed comprised the Hons. James Brown, S. L. Tilley, William Henry Steeves, John M. Johnson, Albert J. Smith, David Wark and Charles Watters. The Hon. Charles Fisher became attorney-general, and, resigning his seat, was reëlected for the county of York prior to the meeting of the legislature on June 24th, 1857. The session lasted only until July 1st, being merely held for the purpose of disposing of the necessary business. James A. Harding was elected speaker of the House, and the legislation was confined to the passage of the supply bills, and matters that were urgent. Tilley took no part in the legislation of this session, for his seat immediately became vacant by his appointment as provincial secretary. The other departments were filled by the appointment of Mr. Brown to the office of surveyor-general; of Mr. Charles Watters, to the office of solicitor-general, and of John M. Johnson as postmaster-general. [186]

The legislature met again on February 10th, 1858, and the speech from the throne dealt mainly with the financial crisis, the Intercolonial Railway, and the progress that was being made in the construction of the line between St. John and Shediac as a part of what was termed the European and North American Railway. The speech also referred to the fact that the surplus civil list fund had been, by arrangement with the British government made the previous year, placed at the disposal of the House of Assembly. It was soon seen that the government was strong in the House, the first test vote being that taken on the passage of the address in reply to the speech from the throne. This came in the form of an amendment, regretting that the arrangement in regard to the surplus civil list fund had been acceded to without the consent of the House. This amendment to the address received the support of only six members. A return brought down at an early period in the session showed that the revenue of the province for the fiscal year, ending October 31st, 1857, amounted to $668,252 an increase of $86,528 over the previous year. Of this sum upwards of $540,000 came from import duties and what were termed railway impost, which was simply duties levied on imports for the purpose of defraying the cost of the railways then building. The casual and territorial revenue yielded only eighteen thousand pounds but the export duties reached almost twenty thousand pounds. [187]

INTERCOLONIAL RAILWAY

The Intercolonial Railway still continued to engage the attention of the legislature, and correspondence with the secretary of state, with the government of Canada, and with the government of Nova Scotia, in regard to this great work, was laid before the House soon after the session opened. The government of New Brunswick consulted with the governments of Canada and Nova Scotia as to what assistance should be given by the imperial government towards the construction of the Intercolonial Railway from Halifax to Quebec, in the form of a guarantee of interest. The British government professed to feel a strong sense of the importance of the object, but thought they would not be justified in applying to parliament for the required guarantee, because the heavy expenditures to which Great Britain had been subjected did not leave them at liberty to pledge its revenue for the purpose of assisting in the construction of public works of this description, however desirable in themselves. The correspondence on the subject of the Intercolonial Railway extended over a period of more than twenty years and grew to enormous proportions, but it is safe to assert that this line of railway would not have been constructed in the nineteenth century but for the fact that it was undertaken by the Canadian Dominion as a work which had to be built for the purpose of carrying out the terms of confederation as set out in the British North America Act (section 145). [188]

The railway to Shediac was finally completed and opened for traffic on August 5th, 1860, its length being one hundred and eight miles. The nineteen miles between Pointe du Chêne and Moncton had been open as early as August, 1857, and the nine miles from St. John to Rothesay, on June 1st, 1858. The railway was opened from St. John to Hampton in June, 1859, and to Sussex in November of the same year. Although the people of the province had abated something of their enthusiasm for railways by the time the St. John and Shediac line was finished, still its opening was a great event, because it was the commencement of a new era in transportation and gave St. John access to the north shore, from which it had previously been practically shut out. Goods could now be sent by means of railway and steamer to Prince Edward Island, and to the New Brunswick ports on the Gulf of St. Lawrence, and a community of interest which did not exist before was thus created between the most remote sections of the province.

The traffic receipts of the complete line were thought to be highly satisfactory; the business for the first three months amounted to about $45,000, and yielded a revenue of $18,000. This was a good showing and gave promise of still better things for the future. It may be interesting to state that in the last year that the railway was operated by the government of the province, the gross receipts amounted to $148,330, and the net receipts to [189] $51,760. The gross and net revenue of the road had shown a steady increase from the first, and although it had been a costly public work the people of the province considered it a good investment. It was only after it had passed into the hands of the government of Canada, and become a part of the Intercolonial Railway, that any colour was given to the accusation that it was an unprofitable line. The railway from St. John to Shediac had always paid well, and probably, if dissociated from its connecting lines, would at this day pay three or four per cent, upon its original cost.

THE BALLOT

The legislation of the province between 1858 and 1861, although it included many useful measures, evolved nothing that calls for particular mention, with the exception of the law which provided for voting by ballot. This was an innovation to which many were opposed, but which the Liberal party very properly considered necessary to the protection of the voter, who was liable to be coerced by his employer, or by those who had financial relations with him. The ballot system introduced by the government was quite imperfect and did not insure absolute secrecy, because it did not provide for an official ballot such as is required in the system of election which now prevails in connection with the choice of members to our Canadian parliament. Yet it was a vast improvement on open voting, not only because it gave the voter a certain degree of protection, but also from the [190] fact that it tended to promote order at elections, and to do away with that riotous spirit which was characteristic of the earlier contests in the province.

UNIVERSITY OF NEW BRUNSWICK

In 1859 an important step was taken for the reorganization of King's College, which by an Act passed in that year, was changed into the University of New Brunswick. There had always been a great deal of dissatisfaction with the college in consequence of its denominational character, and in 1854 an Act was passed empowering the lieutenant-governor to appoint a commission to inquire into the state of King's College, its management and utility, with a view to improving it. The commissioners appointed were the Hon. John H. Gray, the Rev. Egerton Ryerson, J. W. Dawson, the Hon. John S. Saunders and the Hon. James Brown. The report, which was dated December 28th, 1854, was laid before both branches of the legislature in 1855. In 1857 the college council appointed a committee and prepared a draft of a bill which was laid before the legislature. This, with a few slight alterations, was the bill which was passed in 1859 for the establishment of the University of New Brunswick, and in this bill were embodied the principal recommendations of the commissioners appointed in 1854 to enquire into the state of the college. This Act transferred to the University of New Brunswick all the property of King's College and its endowment, and made the university liable for the payment of the debts and the performance of the contracts of [191] King's College. It created a new governing body for the college to be styled the senate, to be appointed by the governor in council, and the president of the college was required to

be a member of that body and also to be a layman. It conferred upon the senate the power of appointing the professors and other officers of the university, except the president, and also the power of
removing them from office, subject to the approval of the governor
in council. It also authorized the senate to fix their salaries. It abolished the professorship of theology and provided for the affiliation
of other institutions with the university, and also for a number of
free scholars. This Act, which was passed in April, 1859, was especially approved by Her Majesty in council on January 25th, 1860.
Thus a new era in the higher education of New Brunswick was
commenced, and a long step was taken towards making the college
more acceptable to the people of that province. Great hopes were
entertained at the time that this liberalizing of the constitution of the
college would lead to a large increase in the number of its students,
and a more general interest in its work, but, unfortunately, as the
sequel showed, these hopes were only partially realized.

During the spring of 1860 circumstances occurred which led to
the resignation of the postmaster-general, the Hon. Charles Connell.
The legislature having adopted the decimal system of currency in
[192] the place of the pounds, shillings and pence which had been
the currency of the province since its foundation, Mr. Connell, in
March, 1860, was authorized to obtain a new set of postage stamps
of the denominations required for use in the postal service of the
province. No person, at that time, thought that a political crisis
would arise out of this order, but it appears that Mr. Connell, guided by the example of presidents and postmasters-general of the
United States, had made up his mind that instead of the likeness of
the queen, which had been upon all the old postage stamps of the
province, the five-cent stamp, the one which would be most in use,
should bear the impress of his own countenance. Accordingly the
Connell postage stamp, which is now one of the rarest and most
costly of all in the lists of collectors, was procured and was ready to
be used, when Mr. Connell's colleagues in the government discovered what was going on and took steps to prevent the new five-cent
stamp from being issued. The correspondence on the subject, which
will be found in the journals of 1861, is curious and interesting; it
ended in the withdrawal of the objectionable stamps and in the
resignation of Mr. Connell, who complained that he had lost the

confidence of his colleagues, and in resigning, charged them with neglecting the affairs of the province. Only a few of the Connell stamps got into circulation, the remainder of the issue being destroyed. Mr. Connell's place as postmaster-general [193] was filled by the appointment of James Steadman.

RESIGNATION OF MR. FISHER

In the early part of 1861 a very important event occurred in connection with the government which produced a lasting effect on provincial politics. Charges were made by a St. John Conservative paper, *The Colonial Empire*, in which it was stated that members of the government and certain Crown lands officials had been purchasing the most desirable and valuable Crown lands of the province for speculative purposes, and that in bringing these lands to sale the government regulations had been violated and the public treasury had suffered. A committee of the House was appointed to investigate these charges, and inquiry established the fact that an official of the Crown lands department had purchased some eight hundred acres. These lands were all bought at public sale, but in the forms of application other names were used, which was a violation of the rules of the department. A portion of the press at the time created a widespread excitement upon this subject, and the services of the official referred to were dispensed with. Some of the supporters of the government also took such ground in reference to the attorney-general, Mr. Fisher, that his retirement from the government became necessary, the accusation against him being that he had negligently permitted some improper sales of Crown lands to be made. It was felt at the time by some that the penalty that [194] was paid by the attorney-general was excessive for the offence; but, under the excitement then existing, it was the only course that could be taken to avoid the defeat of the government. At the general election that followed a few months later, Mr. Fisher was reëlected for the county of York, and later on, after the excitement had passed over, the delinquent Crown lands official was reinstated. At the same election, that took place in 1861, the government was handsomely sustained, after one of the warmest contests that had ever taken place in New Brunswick. Probably the most effective nomination speech ever made by Tilley, during his long political career, was the one then delivered at the court-house, St. John, in his own defence, and in the vindication of his government against the charges made by the Opposition candidates and press.

[195]

CHAPTER V
THE INTERCOLONIAL RAILWAY

The imperfect means of communication between the Maritime Provinces and Canada had long been recognized as a great evil, and very soon after the introduction of railways into England a line of railway was projected to run from St. Andrews, in New Brunswick, to Quebec. The transfer of a considerable tract of territory, which had been believed to be in New Brunswick, to the state of Maine, under the terms of the Ashburton Treaty, gave a check to this enterprise, and financial difficulties afterwards prevented its accomplishment. A more promising scheme was that of a railway from Halifax to Quebec, and this so far received the approval of the British government that an officer of engineers, Major Robinson, was, in 1847, detailed to conduct a survey of the proposed line. As this gentleman was influenced by purely military considerations, his line was carried as far from the United States boundary as possible, and consequently by a very long and circuitous route. During the session of 1852, Attorney-General Street introduced a series of resolutions in the New Brunswick legislature favouring the building of the Intercolonial Railway jointly by Canada, New [196] Brunswick and Nova Scotia, according to terms which had been agreed upon by the delegates of each. This arrangement was that the Intercolonial Railway should be built through the valley of the St. John. These resolutions were carried by a large majority. During the recess, Mr. Chandler, as the representative of New Brunswick, and Mr. Hincks, the representative of Canada, went to London to endeavour to obtain from the British government financial aid to build the Intercolonial Railway. This was refused on the ground that such a work had to be one of military necessity. Further efforts were made in 1855, and again in 1858, to influence the British government in favour of this railway, but without result; the answer of Downing Street being that the heavy expenditure involved in the Crimean War prevented the government from assisting in the construction of public works, such as the Intercolonial Railway, however desirable in themselves.

DELEGATION TO ENGLAND

The effort to secure the construction of the Intercolonial Railway was renewed in 1861. At a meeting of delegates representing Canada, Nova Scotia and New Brunswick, which was held at Quebec on September 30th, it was resolved that the three governments should renew the offers made to the imperial government in 1858 with reference to the Intercolonial Railway, and that the route to be adopted be decided by the imperial government. The Hon. Mr. Tilley, who was at this [197] Quebec meeting, was sent to England as a delegate to confer with the imperial government with regard to the railway, while Nova Scotia was represented by the Hon. Joseph Howe, and Canada, by the Hon. P. M. Vankoughnet. The delegates reached England in November and placed themselves in communication with the Duke of Newcastle, who was then colonial secretary, and they also had interviews with the prime minister, Lord Palmerston, the chancellor of the exchequer, the secretary of war, and the president of the board of trade. While in England, the seizure of the commissioners of the southern confederacy, Messrs. Mason and Slidell, by Commodore Wilkes, on board the British mail steamer *Trent*, produced a crisis in the relations between Great Britain and the United States which seemed likely to lead to a war, and greatly strengthened the position of the delegates, who were able to point out the difficulty involved in defending Canada without a railway to the sea. They presented their views to the colonial secretary in a very ably written state paper, which should have convinced those to whom it was addressed that the railway was an absolute necessity. The delegates estimated the cost of the railway at £3,000,000 sterling, and they asked the imperial government to join in a guarantee of four per cent. interest on this sum, each of the provinces to guarantee £20,000 a year for this purpose and the imperial government, £60,000. This proposal was rejected by the [198] British government, but it offered "an imperial guarantee of interest towards enabling them to raise by public loan, at a moderate rate, the requisite funds for constructing the railway." The British government, therefore, would do nothing for this great work except to indorse the bonds of the provinces to a limited extent, for it was stated in the Duke of Newcastle's letter to the delegates that "the nature and extent of the guarantee must be determined by the particulars of any scheme which the provincial governments may be disposed to found on the present proposal and on the kind of security which they would offer."

Delegates representing the three provinces met in Quebec in September, 1862, to consider this offer, New Brunswick being represented by Messrs. Tilley, Steeves and Mitchell. The delegates from the Maritime Provinces declared their willingness to propose to their respective governments to accept the proposition of the Duke of Newcastle if Canada would bear one-half of the expense of the railway instead of one-third. The Canadian government offered to assume five-twelfths of the liability for the construction and working of the Intercolonial, and to this the delegates for New Brunswick and Nova Scotia had to agree. This imposed a very serious burthen on two provinces, which, between them, had only six hundred thousand inhabitants, and their willingness to assume it shows the interest they took in this great work. [199]

NEGOTIATIONS IN ENGLAND

In pursuance of an arrangement made at this Quebec meeting, delegates from the three provinces went to England to arrange the terms of the guarantee with the British government; the Hon. Mr. Tilley represented New Brunswick, and the Hon. Joseph Howe, Nova Scotia. Mr. Gladstone, who was then chancellor of the exchequer, insisted on a sinking fund being provided, which was to be a first charge on the revenues of the several provinces. This sinking fund was objected to by the colonial delegates, but the only modification in its terms which they were able to obtain was that the sinking fund was not to take precedence of any existing liability. Before leaving England, Messrs. Tilley and Howe prepared and submitted a memorandum to the Duke of Newcastle in which they expressed a hope that Mr. Gladstone might be induced to reconsider the matter of the sinking fund, and that it would not be insisted on. The Canadian delegates left England without an acceptance of the terms proposed by Mr. Gladstone, and without a formal rejection of them. Previous to the meeting of the Canadian parliament, Tilley proceeded to Quebec to urge upon the Canadian government the preparation of the necessary bills to carry out the agreement entered into for the construction of this great railway. He reported to the lieutenant-governor on his return that the government of Canada, for reasons stated, could not then undertake to pass the legislation required, which they greatly regretted, [200] but that they had not abandoned the arrangements for the construction of the railway. The Canadian government's declaration in the course of the session that they had abandoned this important enterprise was, accordingly, a source of great surprise and regret. The governments of New Brunswick and Nova Scotia passed the necessary legislation at the next session, but the government of Canada took no further step in the matter until the confederation negotiations were commenced in 1864.

[201]

CHAPTER VI
THE MOVEMENT FOR MARITIME UNION

We now come down to an event of the greatest interest, in which Mr. Tilley took part, and one of such vast and far-reaching importance that it quite overshadows all the other events of his career. The confederation of the Canadian provinces was, beyond all question, the most notable colonial movement within the British empire since the American Declaration of Independence. It changed at once the whole character of the colonial relations which had subsisted with the mother country, and substituted for a few weak and scattered colonies a powerful Dominion, able to speak with a united voice, and stand as a helpmeet to the nation from which most of its people had sprung. No man, whatever his views as to the wisdom of that political union may have been at the time, can now deny that it was timely and necessary, if the colonies and the mother country were to preserve their connection with each other. It is safe to say that, if confederation had not taken place in 1867, British interests on this continent would have suffered, and possibly some of the colonies would now have been a part of the United States. The policy of separating the colonies from England, [202] which has been so much advocated by many leading public men in the great republic, would have found free scope, and by balancing the interests of one colony against those of another, promoting dissensions and favouring those provinces which were disposed to a closer union with the United States, something might have been done to weaken their connection with the British empire, which is now the glory and the strength of the Dominion of Canada.

The question of the union of the several colonies of British North America was by no means a new one when it came up for final settlement. It had been discussed at a very early period in the history of the provinces, and indeed it was a question which it was quite natural to discuss, for it seemed but reasonable that colonies of the same origin, owing the same allegiance, inhabited by people who differed but little from each other in any respect, and with many commercial interests in common, should form a political union. No doubt it might have been brought earlier to the front as a vital political question but for the fact that the British government, which was most interested in promoting the union of the colonies, took no step towards that end until almost compelled by necessity to move in the matter. The colonial policy of England, as represented by the colonial office and in the royal instructions to colonial governors, has seldom been wise or far-seeing, and the British colonies which [203] now girdle the world, have been built up mainly as the result of private enterprise; for the part taken by the government has, in most cases, been merely to give official sanction to what private individuals have already done, and to assist in protecting British interests when they have become important, especially in new regions of the world.

CONFEDERATION FORESHADOWED

When the Earl of Durham was sent out as governor-general of Canada after the rebellion there in 1838, he suggested in his report that the union of the colonies of British North America was one of the remedies which ought to be resorted to for the pacification of Canada and the reconstruction of its constitution. While a large proportion of the people of the colonies looked with favour upon the idea of a political union, there was in all of them a large body of objectors who were steadily opposed to it. People of that kind are to be found in all countries, and they have existed in all ages of the world's history. They are the persons who see in every new movement a thousand difficulties which cannot be surmounted. Their minds are constructed on the principle of rejecting all new ideas, and clinging to old forms and systems long after they have lost their vitality. They are a class who look back for precedents for any step of a political character which it is proposed to take, and who judge of everything by the standard of some former age. They seem to forget that precedents must be created some time or another, and that the present [204] century has as good a right to create precedents as any of its predecessors. To these people every objection that could be urged against confederation was exaggerated and magnified, and whenever any proposal was made which seemed to tend towards the union of the colonies, their voices were heard upon the other side. We need not doubt the honesty or loyalty of these objectors, or consider that they were unfavourable either to British connection or to the building up of the empire. It was merely their misfortune that they were constitutionally adverse to change, and could not see any merit in a political movement which involved the idea of novelty.

For some time the principal advocate of confederation in the Maritime Provinces was the Hon. Joseph Howe, a man of such ability and force of character that on a wider stage he might have risen to eminence, and ranked amongst the world's great statesmen. [10] It is impossible indeed not to regret that so great a man, one so imperial in his instincts and views, should have been condemned to spend his life within the bounds of one small province.

ATTITUDE OF COLONIAL OFFICE

The question of the political union of the British North American provinces was brought up in the House of Assembly of Nova Scotia in 1854, and then the leaders of both parties, the Hon. Mr. Johnson for the Conservatives, and the Hon. Mr. [205] Howe for the Liberals, united in advocating the measure, and in depicting the advantage which would accrue from it not only to Nova Scotia, but to every British province in North America. In 1858 the question of confederation was discussed in the parliament of Canada, and such a union was made a part of the policy of the government; for Mr. A. T. Galt, on becoming a member of the administration, insisted upon its being made a cabinet question, and Sir Edmund Head, the governor-general, in his speech at the close of the session, intimated that his government would take action in the matter during the recess. Messrs. Cartier, Galt, and Ross, who were in England representing the government of Canada, waited upon the colonial secretary, Sir Edward Bulwer Lytton, asking the authority of the imperial government for a meeting of representatives from each of the colonies to take the question of union into consideration. The colonial secretary informed the Canadian delegates, no doubt after consultation with his colleagues, that the question of confederation was necessarily one of an imperial character, and declined to authorize the meeting, because no expression of sentiment on the subject had as yet been received from any of the Maritime Provinces except Nova Scotia. The Earl of Derby's government fell a few months after this declaration of its policy in regard to the colonies, and was succeeded by the government of Lord Palmerston, which was [206] in office at the time when the negotiations which resulted in the confederation of the colonies were commenced. At first Lord Palmerston's government seems to have been no more favourable to the union of the colonies than its predecessor; for in 1862 the Duke of Newcastle, then colonial secretary, in a despatch to the governor-general of Canada, after stating that Her Majesty's government was not prepared to announce any definite policy on the question of confederation, added that, "If a union, either partial or complete, should hereafter be proposed, with the concurrence of all the provinces to be united, I am sure that the matter would be weighed in this country both by the public, by parliament and by Her Majesty's government, with no other feeling than an anxiety to discern and promote any course which might be the most conducive to the prosperity, strength and harmony of all the British communities of North America." It must always be a subject of astonishment that the British government for so many years should have had no definite policy on a matter so momentous, and that they should have sought to discourage, rather than otherwise, a project which has been of such vast importance to the empire.

The first impulse in favour of confederation in the minds of the members of Lord Palmerston's cabinet seems to have developed about the time when it became evident that the result of the civil war in the United States would be the defeat of [207] the southern confederacy and the consolidation of the power of the great republic in a more effectual union than that which had existed before. No one who was not blind could fail to see that this change of attitude on the part of the United States would demand a corresponding change in the relations of the British colonies towards each other; for from being a mere federation of states, so loosely connected that secession was frequently threatened by states both north and south, the United States, as the result of the war, had become a nation with a strong central government, which had taken to itself powers never contemplated by the constitution, and which added immensely to its offensive and defensive strength.

A MISSIONARY OF UNION

In 1863, Thomas D'Arcy McGee, a member of the Canadian cabinet and a man of great eloquence and ability, visited St. John and delivered a lecture in the Mechanics' Institute Hall on the subject of the union of the colonies. His lecture was fully reported in the *Morning News*, a paper then published in that city, and attracted wide attention because it opened up a subject of the highest interest for the contemplation of the people of the provinces. Shortly afterwards a series of articles on the same subject, written by the author of this book, appeared in the columns of the *Morning News*, and were widely read and quoted. These articles followed closely the lines laid down for the union of the colonies by the late Peter S. Hamilton, [208] of Halifax, a writer of ability whose articles on the subject were collected in pamphlet form and extensively circulated. Thus in various ways the public mind was being educated on the question of confederation, and the opinion that the union of the British North American colonies was desirable was generally accepted by all persons who gave any attention to the subject. It was only when the matter came up in a practical form and as a distinct proposition to be carried into effect, that the violent opposition which was afterwards developed against confederation began to be shown.

An event occurred in the summer of 1864 which had its effect on the question of confederation. Up to that time the people of Canada and New Brunswick had been almost wholly unknown to each other, because the difficulties of travelling between the two provinces were so great. Any person who desired to reach Montreal at that time from St. John had to take the international steamer to Portland, Me., and was then carried by the Grand Trunk Railway to his destination. Quebec could be reached in summer by the steamer from Pictou which called at Shediac, but in winter the journey had to be made by the Grand Trunk Railway from Portland, the only alternative route being the road by which the mails were carried from Edmunston north to the St. Lawrence. Under these circumstances the people of the Canadian provinces and of the Maritime Provinces had but few opportunities [209] of seeing each other, and the people of all the provinces knew much more of their neighbours in the United States than they did of their fellow-colonists. One result of the Hon. D'Arcy McGee's visit in 1863 was an invitation by the city of St. John to the legislature of Canada to visit the Maritime Provinces. The invitation was accepted and a party of about one hundred, comprising members of the legislature, newspaper men, and others, visited St. John in the beginning of August, 1864. Their trip was extended to Fredericton, where they were the guests of the government of New Brunswick, and to Halifax, where they were the guests of that city and of the government of Nova Scotia. This visit produced a good effect upon the public mind, and enabled the Maritime people to see what kind of men their fellow-colonists of Upper and Lower Canada were.

POLITICAL CRISIS IN CANADA

In the meantime a great crisis had arisen in the government of Canada, which was the immediate cause of the active part which that province took in the confederation movement. When Upper and Lower Canada were united in 1841, it was arranged that the representation of each province in the legislature should be equal. The arrangement at that time was favourable to Upper Canada, which had a smaller population than Lower Canada; but in the course of time, as the population of Upper Canada increased faster than that of the lower province, the people of Upper [210] Canada felt that they had less representation than they were entitled to, and this state of affairs led to the raising of the cry of "Representation by Population" which was so often heard in that province prior to the era of confederation. In 1864 Upper Canada had half a million more people than Lower Canada, and yet was only entitled to the same number of members in the legislature. Another serious difficulty, which arose out of the union, was the necessity, which not long afterwards began to be recognized, of the government having a majority in the legislature from each section of the province. This, in time, grew to be so great an evil that the successful government of Canada became almost impossible, for the majority for the government in one province might at any time be disturbed by some local feeling, and as a consequence the government overthrown. To trace the history of the difficulties which arose from this cause would be to recite twenty years of the history of Canada; but it is only necessary to point out thus plainly the reasons for the willingness of the people of Upper and Lower Canada to resort to confederation as a means of getting rid of their embarrassments.

MACDONALD-BROWN COALITION

In 1863, the Hon. John Sandfield Macdonald was leader of the government, but he was compelled to resign when parliament met in the early part of 1864, and in March of that year a new administration under the premiership of Sir E. P. [211] Taché was formed. This new government developed very little strength, and was defeated on June 14th by a vote of fifty-eight to sixty, on a question relative to some transaction connected with bonds of the city of Montreal. A deadlock had come, and as it was evident that no new government which could be formed was likely to command sufficient support, it became necessary to make some new arrangements in regard to the system of administration. Immediately after the defeat of the government, Mr. George Brown, leader of the Opposition, spoke to several supporters of the administration strongly urging that the present time should be availed of for the purpose of settling forever the constitutional difficulties between Upper and Lower Canada, and assuring them that he was prepared to coöperate with the existing or any other administration that would deal with the question promptly and firmly, with a view to its final settlement. After much negotiation Messrs. Brown, Mowat and McDougall, three prominent members of the Reform party, agreed to enter the government for the purpose of carrying out this policy based on a federal union of all the provinces.

SCHEME OF MARITIME UNION

Prior to this time there had been various efforts made by the government of New Brunswick to enter into closer relations with Nova Scotia and Prince Edward Island. Previous to the year 1861 a number of factories of various kinds had been [212] established in the Maritime Provinces, but the limited market they then enjoyed prevented their extension and crippled their operations. To remedy this, Mr. Tilley, with the approval of his colleagues in the government, visited Nova Scotia and Prince Edward Island and proposed to the governments of both provinces free admission of their natural products and a uniform tariff on dutiable goods. In Halifax he had a lengthy and satisfactory conference with Mr. Howe, then leader of the government, and with Dr. Tupper, the leader of the Opposition. Both gentlemen agreed that the proposed arrangements would be in the interests of the three provinces, and Mr. Howe agreed to submit the matter to his government with the view of legislative action at the next session. Mr. Tilley then proceeded to Charlottetown, Prince Edward Island. At the conference held with the government there, his proposal was not so favourably entertained, the objection being that the existing tariff of Prince Edward Island was lower than the tariff of either Nova Scotia or New Brunswick, and sufficient for the financial wants of the Island, and that the necessary advance would be imposing taxation beyond their requirements. Notwithstanding the failure to secure the coöperation of the Island government, it was decided that the joint action of the Nova Scotia and New Brunswick legislatures in the direction named was desirable. When the Nova [213] Scotia legislature met and the public accounts were proposed, it was found that a reduction of tariff was not practicable, and Howe informed Tilley that the scheme would have to be post-poned, "though in other respects desirable." But the subject was not allowed to sleep, and in 1864 there was a renewal of the movement for a union of the Maritime Provinces. At the session of the New Brunswick legislature held that year, resolutions were passed au-thorizing the government to enter into negotiations with Nova Sco-tia and Prince Edward Island to hold a convention for the purpose of carrying such a union into effect. Similar resolutions were carried in the legislatures of Nova Scotia and Prince Edward Island, and the convention thus authorized was appointed to meet at Charlotte-town in the month of September following.

FOOTNOTES:

[10] For a full account of Howe's views on confederation see the Hon. J. W. Longley's *Joseph Howe* in this series.

[215]

CHAPTER VII
THE QUEBEC CONFERENCE

The delegates appointed by the government of New Brunswick for the purpose of representing the provinces at Charlottetown in the convention for a union of the Maritime Provinces, were the Hon. Messrs. Tilley, Steeves, Johnson, Chandler and Gray. The first three were members of the government, while Messrs. Gray and Chandler were leading members of the Opposition, so that the arrangement had the assent of the leaders of both political parties and was in no sense a party movement. The Nova Scotia delegation consisted of the Hon. Charles Tupper, the leader of the government, the attorney-general, Mr. Henry, and Mr. Dickey, a Conservative supporter, and also the Hon. Adams G. Archibald and Jonathan McCully, leaders of the Liberal party. The Prince Edward Island delegates were also chosen from both sides of politics. The convention was opened in due form at Charlottetown on September 8th, in the chamber of the House of Assembly. The delegations had no power to decide finally on any subject, because any arrangements they made were necessarily subject to the approval of the legislatures of the three Maritime Provinces. But at this time the sentiment in favour [216] of maritime union was so strong it was confidently believed that whatever was agreed upon at Charlottetown would become the basis of a future union.

CHARLOTTETOWN CONVENTION

The government of Canada had full knowledge of what was going on at Charlottetown, and they considered the time opportune for the purpose of bringing to the notice of the delegates from the Maritime Provinces the subject of a confederation of all the British North American colonies. A telegram was received while the delegates were in session announcing that representatives of the government of Canada had left Quebec for the purpose of meeting the delegates of the Maritime Provinces, and placing certain proposals before them. On the receipt of this message the further consideration of the question which they had met to discuss was deferred until after the Canadian delegates had arrived. They came in the government steamer *Victoria* on the following day and were found to embrace the leading men then in Canadian political life,—the Hons. J. A. Macdonald, George Brown, Georges E. Cartier, Alexander T. Galt, Thomas D'Arcy McGee, Hector L. Langevin, William McDougall and Alexander Campbell. These delegates represented the Reform, as well as the Conservative party, and were therefore able to speak with authority in regard to the views of the people of both Upper and Lower Canada. They were accorded seats in the convention, and at once submitted [217] reasons why in their opinion a scheme of union, embracing the whole of the British North American colonies, should be adopted. The Hon. John A. Macdonald and Messrs. Brown and Cartier were heard on this subject, the financial position of Canada was explained, and the sources of revenue and wealth of the several provinces were discussed. Speeches were also made by Messrs. Galt, McGee, Langevin and McDougall, and after having commanded the attention of the convention for two days the Canadian deputation withdrew. Before doing so they proposed that if the convention concluded to suspend its deliberations upon the question of Maritime union, they should adjourn to Quebec at an early day, to be named by the governor-general, to consider the question of confederation. On the following day the convention adjourned, on the ground that it would be more for the general interest of British North America to adopt the larger union than a union of the Maritime Provinces merely, and it was thought that this might be effected without any very great difficulty, for there was then no strong feeling evinced in any quarter against confederation.

From Charlottetown the members of the convention and the Canadian deputation went to Halifax, where they were received most cordially and entertained at a banquet. They then took their departure for St. John, where they were entertained at a public dinner at which many leading men of the [218] city were present. The chair was occupied by the Hon. John H. Gray, one of the delegates, and the expressions in favour of the proposed confederation were strong and hearty. No one could have suspected at that time that the movement for confederation would meet with so much opposition in New Brunswick. All seemed plain sailing but, as the result showed, the battle for confederation had yet to be fought, and it was won only after a long and doubtful struggle.

THE QUEBEC CONFERENCE

According to arrangement, the delegations from the other provinces met in convention at Quebec on October 10th, all the colonies, including Newfoundland, were represented and the delegates were as follows: —

Canada. — Hon. Sir Etienne P. Taché, premier; Hon. John A. Macdonald, attorney-general west; Hon. Georges E. Cartier, attorney-general east; Hon. George Brown, president of the executive council; Hon. Alexander T. Galt, finance minister; Hon. Alexander Campbell, commissioner of Crown lands; Hon. William McDougall, provincial secretary; Hon. Thomas D'Arcy McGee, minister of agriculture; Hon. Hector Langevin, solicitor-general east; Hon. J. Cockburn, solicitor-general west; Hon. Oliver Mowat, postmaster-general; Hon. J. C. Chapais, commissioner of public works.

Nova Scotia. — Hon. Charles Tupper, provincial secretary; Hon. W. A. Henry, attorney-general, [219] Hon. R. B. Dickey, Hon. Adams G. Archibald, Hon. Jonathan McCully.

New Brunswick. — Hon. Samuel L. Tilley, provincial secretary; Hon. John M. Johnson, attorney-general; Hon. Edward B. Chandler, Hon. John Hamilton Gray, Hon. Peter Mitchell, Hon. Chas. Fisher, Hon. William H. Steeves.

Newfoundland. — Hon. F. B. T. Carter, speaker of the House of Assembly; Hon. Ambrose Shea.

Prince Edward Island. — Hon. John Hamilton Gray, premier; Hon. Edward Palmer, attorney-general; Hon. W. H. Pope, provincial secretary; Hon. George Coles, Hon. A. A. Macdonald, Hon. T. H. Haviland, Hon. Edward Whelan.

Sir Etienne P. Taché, who was then premier of Canada, was unanimously chosen president of the conference, and Major Hewitt Bernard, of the staff of the attorney-general west, private and confidential secretary. It was arranged that the convention should hold its meetings with closed doors, and it was laid down as a principle of the discussion that, as the matters to come up for debate were all of a novel character, no man should be prejudiced or held liable to the charge of inconsistency because he had changed his views in regard to any particular matter in the course of the discussion. It was also agreed that the vote, in case of a division, should be by provinces and not by numbers, Canada having two votes, representing Canada East and Canada West, and each [220] of the other provinces one. This arrangement made it quite certain that the interests of the Maritime Provinces were not likely to be prejudiced by the result of the vote, or the work of the convention. It was soon decided that a federal union was to be preferred to a legislative union, and on the second day of the meeting the outlines of the proposed confederation were submitted in a series of resolutions by the Hon. John A. Macdonald. The general model of the proposed confederation was that of the United States, but with this difference, that whereas in the United States all powers not expressly given by the constitution to the federal government are held to belong to the several states, in the Canadian constitution all powers not expressly reserved to the several provinces were held to belong to the federal parliament. Thus in the United States the residuum of power is in the several states, while in Canada it is in the federal union and in the parliament of the Dominion. No doubt the recent example of the civil war in the United States, which was the result of an extreme assertion of state rights, was largely responsible for this feature of the Canadian constitution. It is clear, however, that it is a feature that is to be commended, because its tendency is to cause Canadians to regard themselves rather as Canadians than as belonging to any particular province, while in the United States the feeling of statehood is still very strong. There are, [221] of course, many other contrasts between the Canadian confederation and the federal union of the United States, arising from radical differences in the system of government. Nothing like responsible government, as understood in the British empire, exists in the United States, while this essential feature had to be preserved in the Canadian constitution, not only with reference to the Dominion parliament, but also in the legislatures of the several provinces.

DIFFICULT QUESTIONS

In all the proceedings at Quebec, Mr. Tilley, as the finance minister of New Brunswick, took a very prominent part. One great difficulty which arose was with respect to the amount of money to be given by the federal government to the several provinces for legislative purposes, in lieu of the revenue which they had been accustomed to obtain from customs duties and otherwise. The whole customs establishment was to be transferred to the central government, and as most of the provinces would have no other means of obtaining a revenue except by direct taxation, this feature of the matter became of very vital importance. The difficulty was increased by the fact that by the municipal system prevailing in Upper Canada the local needs of the municipalities, in the way of roads, bridges, schools and other matters, were provided for by local taxation, whereas in the Maritime Provinces the provincial government had been accustomed to bear these burdens. It was therefore an essential [222] requisite to any scheme of union, to make it acceptable to the people of the Maritime Provinces, that sufficient money should be given to the provincial governments to enable them to continue these services as before. It was difficult to convince the representatives of Upper Canada of this, and it appears that the conference nearly broke up without arriving at any result, simply because of the apparently irreconcilable differences of opinion between the representatives of the Maritime Provinces and those of Canada in regard to this point. Finally these differences were overcome, and the conclusions of the conference were embodied in a series of seventy-two resolutions, which were agreed to, and which were to be authenticated by the signatures of the delegates, and transmitted to their respective governments, and also to the governor-general, for the secretary of state for the colonies. These resolutions formed the first basis of confederation and became what is known as the Quebec scheme.

It was perhaps inevitable that during the discussion of the scheme of confederation by the Quebec convention, the proceedings should be secret, but this restriction should have been removed as soon as the convention adjourned. That this was not done was the principal reason for the very unfavourable reception which the Quebec scheme met with from the people of New Brunswick, when it was placed before them. It was agreed [223] at the Quebec conference that the scheme should not be made public until after the delegates had reported to their respective governments for their approval, but it was impossible that a document, the terms of which were known to so many men, should be kept wholly concealed from the public, and so the details of the scheme leaked out and soon became a topic for public discussion. These discussions would have been conducted in a much more friendly spirit if the Quebec scheme had been given freely to the world, but as it was, prejudices and jealousies, in many cases, darkened the question, and made men, who were otherwise favourable to confederation, assume an attitude of hostility to the Quebec scheme.

SUBVENTIONS TO THE PROVINCES

One of the points which at once attracted the attention of the opponents of the scheme was the sum allowed to the several provinces for the purpose of conducting their local affairs. As the provinces had to surrender to the general government their right to levy customs and excise duties, it became necessary to make up in some way a sum sufficient to enable them to carry on those services which were still left to the provincial legislatures. It was arranged that this sum should be eighty cents a head of the population of the provinces as established by the census of 1861, which would give to New Brunswick something more than two hundred thousand dollars. This feature of the confederation scheme was eagerly seized upon as being [224] a convenient club with which to strike it down. The cry was at once raised that the people of New Brunswick were asked to sell themselves to Canada for the sum of eighty cents a head, and this parrot-like cry was repeated with variations throughout the whole of the election campaign which followed in New Brunswick. It has often been found that a cry of this kind, which is absolutely meaningless, is more effective than the most weighty arguments, for the purpose of influencing men's minds, and this proved to be the case in New Brunswick, when the question of confederation was placed before the people. It was conveniently forgotten by those who attacked the scheme in this fashion that, if the people of New Brunswick were selling themselves to Canada for the sum of eighty cents a head, the people of Canada were likewise selling themselves to New Brunswick for the same sum, because the amount set apart for the provincial legislatures was precisely the same in each case. It would not, however, have suited the enemies of the confederation scheme to view the matter in this light; what was wanted was a cry which would be effective for the purpose of injuring the scheme and making it distasteful to the people who were asked to vote upon it.

OPPONENTS OF CONFEDERATION

It is not necessary to assume that those who opposed confederation were all influenced by sinister motives. Many honest and good men, whose attachment to British institutions could not be questioned, [225] were opposed to it because their minds were of a conservative turn, and because they looked with distrust upon such a radical change that would alter the relations which existed between the province and the mother country. Many, for reasons which it is not easy to understand, were distrustful of the politicians of Canada, whom they looked upon as of less sterling honesty than their own, and some actually professed to believe that the Canadians expected to make up their financial deficits by drawing on the many resources of the Maritime Provinces through the confederation scheme. On the other hand confederation was opposed in the province of New Brunswick by a number of men who could only be described as adventurers, or discredited politicians, and who saw in this contest a convenient way of restoring themselves to influence and power. There were also among the opponents of the scheme some men who recognized in its success the means of perpetuating British power on this continent, and who, being annexationists, naturally looked with aversion upon it for that reason. The vast majority of the people, however, had given the matter but the slightest degree of attention, and their votes were cast in accordance with prejudice hastily formed, which they had an opportunity of reconsidering before another year and a half had elapsed.

FEELING IN NEW BRUNSWICK

It had been arranged at the convention that the first trial of the scheme before the people should be [226] made in New Brunswick, the legislature of which was about expiring, and accordingly the appeal was made to the people and the elections came on in the month of March, 1865. The enemies of confederation were very active in every part of the province, and they left no stone unturned to defeat the measure. The great cry upon which they based their opposition to the union with Canada was that of taxation, and, as the voters of New Brunswick were not inclined to favour any policy which involved high taxation, the appeals made in this way had a powerful effect. All through the rural constituencies the Opposition candidates told the electors that if they united themselves with Canada direct taxation would be the immediate result. They said that every cow, every horse, and every sheep which they owned would be taxed, and that even their poultry would not escape the grasp of the Canadian tax-gatherers. In the city of St. John, Mr. Tilley and his colleague, Mr. Charles Watters, were opposed by Mr. J. V. Troop and Mr. A. B. Wetmore. Mr. Troop was a wealthy ship-owner, whose large means made him an acceptable addition to the strength of the anti-confederate party, although previously he had taken no active part in political affairs. Mr. Wetmore was a lawyer of standing in St. John, who was considered to be one of the best *nisi prius* advocates at the bar, and who carried the methods of the bar largely into his politics. In the course of time he became attorney-general [227] of the province, and later on a judge of the supreme court. Mr. Wetmore, when haranguing St. John audiences, used to depict the dreadful effects of confederation in a manner peculiarly his own. His great plea was an imaginary dialogue between himself and his little son, that precocious infant asking him in lisping tones, "Father, what country do we live in?" to which he would reply, "My dear son, you have no country, for Mr. Tilley has sold us to the Canadians for eighty cents a head."

In the county of St. John, the Hon. John. H. Gray, Charles N. Skinner, W. H. Scovil and James Quinton, who ran as supporters of confederation, were opposed by John W. Cudlip, T. W. Anglin, the Hon. R. D. Wilmot and Joseph Coram. Mr. Cudlip was a merchant, who at one time enjoyed much popularity in the city of St. John. Mr. Anglin was a clever Irishman, a native of the county of Cork, who had lived several years in St. John and edited a newspaper called the *Freeman*, which enjoyed a great popularity among his co-religionists. He was admitted to be the leader of the Irish Catholics of St. John, and had acquired an ascendency over them which was not easily shaken; yet he was not, as a politician, a great success, nor did his efforts to improve the condition of his countrymen always lead to satisfactory results. The Hon. R. D. Wilmot had been a prominent Conservative politician, but was defeated, and had retired to his [228] farm at Belmont. For some years he had been devoting his abilities to stock-raising; but at the first note of alarm on the confederation question he abandoned his agricultural pursuits and rushed into the field to take part in the contest. Mr. Joseph Coram was a leading Orangeman, and a highly respected citizen.

A CRITICAL ELECTION

In the county of York, the Hon. George L. Hatheway, who was then chief commissioner of the board of works, appeared in the field as an Opposition candidate, in company with John C. Allen, John J. Fraser and William H. Needham. Mr. Hatheway deserted the government in its hour of need, apparently because he judged from the cries that were raised against confederation that the current of public opinion was strongly adverse to the Quebec scheme. Having left Mr. Tilley in the lurch on the eve of the confederation contest, he deserted the Smith government sixteen months later, when the second confederation election came to be run, thereby inflicting upon them a blow from which it was impossible they could recover. William H. Needham, whose name has already appeared in this volume, did not lay claim to any high political principles; but having retired some time before to private life, he found in the confederation struggle a good opportunity of getting into the legislature. He was a man of very considerable ability, and had his principles been only equal to his knowledge and talents, he might have risen to the highest position [229] in the province. But his course on many occasions made the public distrustful of him, and he died without having enjoyed any of those honours which men of far less ability have obtained. John James Fraser, afterwards governor of New Brunswick, was a man of a different stamp, and seems to have been a sincere opponent of confederation from conviction. The same may be said of John C. Allen, afterwards chief-justice of the province, a man whose sterling honesty has never been questioned.

[231]

CHAPTER VIII
DEFEAT OF CONFEDERATION

The result of the election was the most overwhelming defeat that ever overtook any political party in the province of New Brunswick. Out of forty-one members, the friends of confederation succeeded in returning only six, the Hon. John McMillan and Alexander C. DesBrisay, for the county of Restigouche; Abner R. McClelan and John Lewis for the county of Albert; and William Lindsay and Charles Connell for the county of Carleton. Every member of the government who held a seat in the House of Assembly, with the exception of the Hon. John McMillan, the surveyor-general, was defeated. The majorities against the confederation candidates in some of the counties were so large it seemed hopeless to expect that any future election would reverse the verdict. Both the city and county of St. John, and the county of York, made a clean sweep, and returned solid delegations of anti-confederates. With the exception of the two Carleton members, the entire block of counties on the River St. John and the county of Charlotte, forming the most populous and best settled part of the province, declared against the Quebec scheme. On the north shore, Westmorland, Kent, Northumberland and [232] Gloucester pronounced the same verdict, and, on the day after the election, the strongest friends of confederation must have felt that nothing but a miracle could ever bring about a change in the opinion which had been pronounced with such emphasis and by so overwhelming a majority. Yet fifteen months later the verdict of March, 1865, was completely reversed, and the anti-confederates were beaten almost as badly as the advocates of confederation had been in the first election; such are the mutations of public opinion.

Mr. Tilley and his colleagues resigned immediately after the result of the elections became known, and the Hon. Albert J. Smith was called upon to form a new government. Mr. Smith had been attorney-general in Mr. Tilley's government up to the year 1862, when he resigned in consequence of a difference with his colleagues in regard to the negotiations which were being carried on for the construction of the Intercolonial Railway. He was a fine speaker, and a man of ability. At a later period, when confederation had been established, he became a cabinet minister in the government of the

Hon. Alexander Mackenzie. His powerful influence was largely responsible for the manner in which the North Shore counties declared against confederation, and he also did much to discredit the Quebec scheme by his speeches delivered in the city of St. John. Mr. Smith did not take the office of attorney-general in the new government, but contented himself with the [233] position of president of the council, the Hon. John C. Allen, of York, becoming attorney-general, and the Hon. A. H. Gillmor, of Charlotte, provincial secretary. The Hon. Bliss Botsford, of Westmorland, was made surveyor-general; and the Hon. George L. Hatheway retained his old office as the chief commissioner of the board of works. The other members of the government were the Hon. Robert Duncan Wilmot, of Sunbury, the Hon. T. W. Anglin, of St. John, and the Hon. Richard Hutchinson, of Miramichi.

THE NEW GOVERNMENT

The new government looked strong and imposing, and seemed to be secure against the assaults of its enemies, yet it was far from being as compact and powerful as it appeared to the outward observer. In the first place, it had the demerit of being founded solely on a negative, and upon opposition to a single line of policy. The reason why these men were assembled together in council as a government was that they were opposed to confederation, and, this question having been disposed of, they were free to differ upon all other points which might arise. Some of the men who thus found themselves sitting together at the same council board had all their lives been politically opposed to each other. The Hon. R. D. Wilmot, an old Conservative, could have little or no sympathy with Mr. A. H. Gillmor, a very strong Liberal. The Hon. A. J. Smith, also a Liberal, had little in common with his attorney-general, Mr. Allen, who was a Conservative. Mr. Odell, the postmaster-general, [234] represented the old Family Compact more thoroughly than any other man who could have been chosen to fill a public office in New Brunswick, for his father and grandfather had held the office of provincial secretary for the long term of sixty years. As he was a man of no particular capacity, and had no qualification for high office, and as he was, moreover, a member of the legislative council, his appointment to such a position was extremely distasteful to many who were strongly opposed to confederation. The Hon. Bliss

Botsford, of Moncton, who became surveyor-general, was another individual who added no strength to the government. In a cabinet consisting of four men in the government who might be classed as Liberals, and five who might be properly described as Conservatives, room was left for many differences and quarrels over points of policy, to say nothing of patronage, after the great question of confederation had been disposed of. Local feelings also were awakened by the make-up of the government, for the North Shore people could not but feel that their interests were in danger of being neglected, as instead of having the attorney-generalship and the surveyor-generalship, which had been theirs in the previous government, they had to be content with a single member in the government, without office, in the person of Mr. Richard Hutchinson, who, as the representative of Gilmour, Rankine & Co., the great lumber house of the North Shore, was extremely [235] unpopular, even in the county which had elected him. The Hon. Robert Duncan Wilmot was perhaps the most dissatisfied man of any, with the new cabinet in which he found himself. He had not been a fortnight in the government before he began to realize the fact that his influence in it was quite overshadowed by that of Mr. Smith and Mr. Anglin, although neither of them held any office. Mr. Wilmot was a man of ability, and of strong and resolute will, so that this condition of affairs became very distasteful to him and his friends, and led to consequences of a highly important character.

DISSENSIONS IN THE GOVERNMENT

The new government had not been long in existence before rumours of dissensions in its ranks became very common. Mr. Wilmot made no secret to his friends of his dissatisfaction, and it was understood that other members found their position equally unpleasant. An element of difficulty was early introduced by the resignation of the chief-justice, Sir James Carter, who, in September, 1865, found it necessary, in consequence of failing health, to retire from the bench, rendering it immediately necessary for the government to fill his place. The Hon. Albert J. Smith, the leader of the government, had he chosen, might have then taken the vacant position, but he did not desire to retire from political life at that time, and the Hon. John C. Allen, his attorney-general, was appointed to the bench as a puisne judge, while the Hon. Robert Parker [236] was made chief-justice. The latter, however, had but few weeks to enjoy his new position, dying in November of the same year, and leaving another vacancy on the bench to be filled. Again, as before, the Hon. Mr. Smith declined to go on the bench, and the Hon. John W. Weldon, who had been a long time a member of former legislatures, and was at one time Speaker, was appointed to the puisne judgeship, and the Hon. William J. Ritchie was made chief-justice. The entire fitness of the latter for the position of chief-justice made his appointment a popular one, but he was the junior of the Hon. Lemuel A. Wilmot as a judge, and the Hon. R. D. Wilmot, who was a cousin of the latter, thought the senior judge should have received the appointment of chief-justice. His disappointment at the office being given to another caused a very bad feeling on his part towards the government, and he would have resigned his seat forthwith but for the persuasions of some of those who were not friends of the government, who intimated to him that he could do them a great deal more damage by retaining his seat, and resigning at the proper time than by abandoning the government at that moment. Mr. Wilmot remained in the government until January, 1866, but although of their number, his heart was estranged from them, and he may properly be regarded as an enemy in their camp.

CONFEDERATION VICTORY IN YORK

Mr. Anglin also had some difference with his colleagues with regard to railway matters, and he [237] resigned his seat early in November, 1865; still he gave a general support to the government, although no longer in its councils. But the most severe blow which the administration received arose from the election in the county of York, which followed the seating of the Hon. John C. Allen on the bench. The confederation party had been so badly beaten in York at the general election that no doubt was felt by the government that any candidate they might select would be chosen by a very large majority. The candidate selected by the government to contest York was Mr. John Pickard, a highly respectable gentleman, who was engaged in lumbering, and who was extremely popular in that county, in consequence of his friendly relations with all classes of the community and the amiability of his disposition. The Hon. Charles Fisher was brought forward by the confederation party as their candidate in York, although the hope of defeating Mr. Pickard seemed to be desperate, for at the previous election Mr. Fisher had received only 1,226 votes against 1,799 obtained by Mr. Needham, who stood lowest on the poll among the persons elected for York. Mr. Fisher by his efforts in the York campaign, which resulted in his election, struck a blow at the anti-confederate government from which it never recovered. His election was the first dawn of light and hope to the friends of confederation in New Brunswick, for it showed clearly enough that whenever the people of the province were given [238] another opportunity of expressing their opinion on the question of confederation, their verdict would be a very different one from that which they had given at the general election. Mr. Fisher beat Mr. Pickard by seven hundred and ten votes, receiving seven hundred and one votes more than at the general election, while Mr. Pickard's vote fell five hundred and seventy-two below that which Mr. Needham had received on the same occasion.

[239]

CHAPTER IX
TILLEY AGAIN IN POWER

Among the causes that had assisted to defeat confederation in New Brunswick, when the question was first placed before the people, was the active hostility of the lieutenant-governor, Mr. Arthur Hamilton Gordon, a son of that Earl of Aberdeen who was prime minister of England at the outbreak of the Crimean War. Mr. Gordon had been a strong advocate of maritime union and had anticipated that he would be the first governor of the united province of Acadia, or by whatever name the maritime union was to be known. He was therefore greatly disappointed and annoyed when the visit of the Canadians to Charlottetown, in September, 1864, put an end to the conference which had met for the purpose of arranging the terms of a union of that character. While a governor cannot take a very active part in political matters, he may stimulate others to hostility or to a certain course of action, who, under other circumstances, would be neutral or inactive, and there is reason to believe that some of the men who were most prominent in opposing confederation at the general election of 1865 were mainly influenced by the views of the lieutenant-governor. Confederation, [240] however, had been approved by the British government, after the terms arranged at Quebec had been submitted to it in a despatch from the governor-general; and those officials in New Brunswick and elsewhere, who expected to find support in Downing Street in their hostility to confederation, were destined to be greatly disappointed. Not long after the new government was formed in New Brunswick, Mr. Gordon returned to England, and it was generally believed that he was sent for by the home authorities. Instead of being favourably received on the ground of his opposition to confederation, he is said to have been compelled to submit to a stern reproof for his anti-constitutional meddling in a matter which did not concern him, and to have been given decidedly to understand that if he returned to New Brunswick, to fill out the remainder of his term of office, it must be as one pledged to assist in carrying out confederation and not to oppose it. When Mr. Gordon returned he was an entirely changed man, and whatever influence he was able to exert from that time forward was used in favour of confederation.

FENIAN THREATS

Another cause which made confederation more acceptable to the people of the province arose from the threats of the Fenians to invade Canada, which were made during the year 1865, and which were followed by armed invasions during the following year. Although there was no good reason for believing that the opponents of confederation were [241] less loyal than its supporters or less inclined to favour British connection, it was remarked that all the enemies of British connection seemed to have got into the anti-confederate camp. The Fenian movement had its origin in the troubles in Ireland arising out of oppressive land laws and other local causes, and it soon extended to America, where the politicians found it useful as a means of increasing their strength among the Irish people. At that time, there were in the United States many hundreds of thousands of men who had been disbanded from the army at the close of the Civil War, and who were only too ready to embrace any new opportunity of winning for themselves fame and rank on other fields of glory. Among these disbanded soldiers were many Irishmen, and it soon came to be known that bands of men could be collected in the United States for the invasion of this country, with the avowed object of driving the British flag from the American continent and substituting the stars and stripes. It was impossible that the people of Canada could view without emotion these preparations for their undoing, and in New Brunswick, especially, which was the first province to be threatened, the Fenian movement materially assisted in deciding the manner in which the people should vote on this great question of confederation when it came to be submitted to them a second time.

The House of Assembly met on March 8th, [242] 1866, and the speech from the throne, delivered by the lieutenant-governor, contained the following paragraph: "I have received Her Majesty's commands to communicate to you a correspondence on the affairs of British North America, which has taken place between Her Majesty's principal secretary of state for the colonies and the governor-general of Canada; and I am further directed to express to you the strong and deliberate opinion of Her Majesty's government that it is an object much to be desired that all the British North American colonies should agree to unite in one government. These papers will immediately be laid before you." This paragraph was not inserted in the speech without considerable pressure on the part of the lieutenant-governor, and it excited a great deal of comment at the time, because it seemed to endorse the principle of confederation, although emanating from a government which had been placed in power as the result of an election in which confederation had been condemned. When this portion of the speech was read by the lieutenant-governor, in the legislative council chamber, the crowd outside the bar gave a hearty cheer, — a circumstance which never occurred before in the province of New Brunswick, and perhaps not in any other British colony.

The members of the House favourable to confederation immediately took up the matter, and dealt with it as if the government had thereby [243] pledged themselves in favour of that policy, and indeed there was a fair excuse for such an inference. When the secret history of the negotiations between the lieutenant-governor and his advisers, prior to the meeting of the legislature, comes to be told, it will be found that at least some of the members of the government had given His Excellency to understand that they were prepared to reverse their former action and to adopt confederation. The difficulty with them was that they feared their own supporters, and thought that if they made such a move they would lose the favour of those who had placed them in power, and this fear was certainly a very natural one.

DESERTED BY FRIENDS

As soon as the House met, it was discovered that Mr. A. R. Wetmore, one of the prominent supporters of the government who had been elected to represent the city of St. John as an anti-confederate, was no longer in sympathy with the government. Mr. Wetmore's long experience as a *nisi prius* lawyer, and his curt and imperturbable manner, rendered him a most exasperating and troublesome opponent, and at a very early period of the session he commenced to make it unpleasant for his former friends. He cross-examined the members of the government in the fashion which he had learned from long experience in the courts. Such attacks proved extremely damaging as well as very annoying.

The address in reply to the speech from the throne was moved in the House of Assembly by [244] Colonel Boyd, of Charlotte County, and when the paragraph relating to confederation was read, Mr. Fisher asked him what it meant. Mr. Boyd replied that the government had no objection to confederation, provided the terms were satisfactory. This reply still further strengthened the feeling that the government were inclined to pass the measure which they had been elected to oppose. Mr. Fisher moved an amendment to the fourth paragraph of the address, which referred to the Fenian conspiracy against British North America, expressing the opinion that while His Excellency might rely with confidence on the cordial support of the people for the protection of the country, his constitutional advisers were not by their general conduct entitled to the confidence of the legislature. This amendment was seconded by Mr. DesBrisay, of Kent, who had been elected as a supporter of the government, and it was debated at great length. The discussion upon it continued from day to day for about three weeks, when, on April 10th, the government resigned in consequence of difficulties with His Excellency in regard to his reply to the address of the legislative council. The legislative council had proceeded to pass the address in reply to the speech, but in consequence of the delay in the House of Assembly, this reply had not before been presented to the governor. In answer to the address of the legislative council, His Excellency said: "I will immediately transmit your address to the secretary [245] of state for the colonies in order that it may be laid at the foot of the throne. Her Majesty the Queen has already been pleased to express deep interest in a closer union of her North America colonies and will no doubt greatly appreciate this decided expression of your opinion, and the avowal of your desire that all British North America should unite in one community, under one strong and efficient government, which cannot but tend to hasten the accomplishment of this great measure."

THE GOVERNMENT RESIGNS

The resignation of the government was announced in the House of Assembly on April 13th by the Hon. A. J. Smith, and the correspondence between the lieutenant-governor and his advisers was laid before the House at the same time. The immediate and ostensible cause of the resignation was the terms of approval in which the lieutenant-governor had replied to the address of the legislative council in reference to confederation. Mr. Smith claimed that it was the duty of the lieutenant-governor to consult his constitutional advisers in regard to the answer to be given, and that, in assuming to himself the right to reply to such an address without consulting them, he had not acted in accordance with the true spirit of the constitution. This was certainly sound doctrine, and the reply of the lieutenant-governor was by no means satisfactory on this point, but he was able to show that Mr. Smith had himself expressed his willingness to enter into a scheme of union, although [246] opposed to the Quebec scheme, and had suggested that, as a preliminary step, the papers on that subject should be referred to a joint committee of both Houses with an understanding that the committee should report in favour of a measure of union. At a later period Mr. Smith seemed indisposed to carry out this arrangement, his conduct evidently being the result of timidity, and so he found himself, to use the language of Sir Arthur Gordon, "entangled in contradictory pledges from which he found it impossible to extricate himself." He had, in fact, placed himself in the power of the lieutenant-governor, and his only resource was to resign. It was understood at the time, and has never been denied, that His Excellency was acting under the advice of the Hon. Peter Mitchell, a member of the legislative council, who was a strong supporter of confederation. Mr. Mitchell was a man of great force of character, and, next to Mr. Tilley, must be regarded as the most potent factor in bringing about the change in the sentiments of the people of the province with respect to confederation.

The lieutenant-governor called upon the Hon. Peter Mitchell, who was a member of the legislative council, to form a government. Mr. Mitchell had been very active in the cause of confederation, and was the moving spirit in the legislative council in all the proceedings in its favour taken in that body; but, when asked to form a new government, he advised the lieutenant-governor that the proper [247] person to undertake that responsibility was the Hon. Mr. Tilley. The latter, however, declined the task on the ground that he was not a member of the legislature, whereupon Mr. Mitchell associated with himself the Hon. Mr. Wilmot for the purpose of forming a new government. The government was announced on April 18th, and was formed as follows:—Hon. Peter Mitchell, president of the council; Hon. S. L. Tilley, provincial secretary; Hon. Charles Fisher, attorney-general; Hon. Edward Williston, solicitor-general; Hon. John McMillan, postmaster-general; Hon. A. R. McClelan, chief commissioner of public works; Hon. R. D. Wilmot and Hon. Charles Connell, members without office. The latter afterwards became surveyor-general.

THE FENIAN INVASION

While the government was being formed in New Brunswick, a Fenian army was gathering upon the border for the purpose of invading the province. This force consisted of four or five hundred young men, most of whom had been in the army of the United States. It was recruited at New York, and its chief was a Fenian named Doran Killian. A part of his force arrived at Eastport on April 10th, and a schooner, laden with arms for the Fenians, soon after reached that place. From this schooner, which was seized by the United States authorities, one hundred and seventeen cases of arms and ammunition were taken,—a clear proof that the intentions of the Fenians were warlike, and that their presence on [248] the border was not a mere demonstration. The Fenians appeared to have been under the impression—as many residents of the United States are to this day—that the people of Canada and of New Brunswick were dissatisfied with their own form of government, and were anxious to come under the protection of the stars and stripes. This absurd idea was responsible, largely, for the War of 1812, and it has been responsible, since then, for many other movements, with respect to the British provinces of North America, in which residents of the United States have taken part. There never was a greater delusion than this, and, in the instance referred to, the Fenians were doomed to be speedily undeceived. The presence of a Fenian force on the border sounded like a bugle blast to every able-bodied man in New Brunswick, and the call for troops to defend the country was instantly responded to. About one thousand men were called out and marched to the frontier. The troops called out consisted of the three batteries of the New Brunswick regiment of artillery, seven companies of the St. John volunteer battalion, one company of the first battalion of the York County militia, one company each of the first and third battalions of the Charlotte County militia, and two companies each of the second and fourth battalions of the Charlotte County militia. These troops remained in arms on the frontier for nearly three months, and were disbanded by a general order dated June 20th. The [249] Fenian raid on New Brunswick proved to be a complete fiasco. The frontier was so well guarded by the New Brunswick militia and by British soldiers, and the St. Croix so thoroughly patrolled by British warships, that the Fenians had no opportunity to make any impression upon the province. It ought to be added that the United States government was prompt to take steps to prevent any armed invasion, and General Meade was sent down to Eastport with a force of infantry and a ship of war to prevent the Fenians from making that place a base of operations against these provinces.

CONFEDERATION VICTORIES

The general elections to decide whether or not New Brunswick was willing to become confederated with Canada, were held in May and June. The first election was that for the county of Northumberland on May 25th, and the result was that the four candidates who favoured confederation, Messrs. Johnson, Sutton, Kerr and Williston, were elected by large majorities. The same result followed in the county of Carleton, where the election was held on May 26th, Messrs. Connell and Lindsay being elected by a vote of more than two to one over their anti-confederate opponents. The third election was in Albert County on the 29th, and there Messrs. McClelan and Lewis, the two candidates in favour of confederation, were triumphantly returned. On May 31st, elections were held in Restigouche and Sunbury, and, in these counties, the candidates in favour of confederation were returned by large [250] majorities. The York election came next. In that county, the anti-confederates had placed a full ticket in the field, the candidates being Messrs. Hatheway, Fraser, Needham and Brown. Mr. Fisher had with him on the ticket, Dr. Dow and Messrs. Thompson and John A. Beckwith. Every person expected a vigorous contest in York, notwithstanding the victory of Mr. Fisher over Mr. Pickard a few months before. But, to the amazement of the anti-confederates in other parts of the province, the Hon. George L. Hatheway and Dr. Brown retired after nomination day and left Messrs. Fraser and Needham to do battle alone. Mr. Hatheway's retirement at this time was a deathblow to the hopes of the anti-confederates all over New Brunswick, affecting not only the result in the county of York, but in every other county in which an election was to be held. A few nights before his resignation, Mr. Hatheway had been in St. John addressing a packed meeting of anti-confederates in the hall of the Mechanics' Institute, and he had spoken on that occasion with apparent confidence. When his friends in St. John, who had been so much moved by his vigorous eloquence, learned that he had deserted them, their indignation was extreme, and they felt that matters must indeed be in a bad way when he did not dare to face the York electors.

The election in the county of St. John was held on June 6th, and that in the city, on the seventh. [251] For the county, the confederate candidates were Messrs. C. N. Skinner, John H. Gray, James Quinton and R. D. Wilmot, and the anti-confederate candidates were Messrs. Coram, Cudlip, Robertson and Anglin. The former were elected by very large majorities, Mr. Wilmot, who stood lowest on the poll among the confederates, having a majority of six hundred over Mr. Coram, who stood highest among the defeated candidates. The election for the city was an equally emphatic declaration in favour of confederation. The candidates were the Hon. S. L. Tilley and A. R. Wetmore on the confederate side, and J. V. Troop and S. R. Thompson opposed to confederation. Mr. Tilley's majority over Mr. Troop, who stood highest on the poll of the two defeated candidates, was seven hundred and twenty-six. The only counties which the anti-confederate party succeeded in carrying were Westmorland, Gloucester and Kent, — three counties in which the French vote was very large, — so that of the forty-one members returned, only eight were opponents of confederation. The victory was as complete as that which had been recorded against confederation in the beginning of 1865.

THE BATTLE IS WON

The battle of confederation had been won, and the triumph was mainly due to the efforts of the Hon. Mr. Tilley. That gentleman, as soon as the defeat of confederation took place in March, 1865, had commenced a campaign for the purpose of educating the people on the subject. Being free from his [252] official duties and having plenty of time on his hands, he was able to devote himself to the work of explaining the advantages of the proposed union to the people of the province; and during the years 1865 and 1866, he spoke in almost every county on the subject which was so near to his heart. He had embraced confederation with a sincere desire for the benefit of his native province, and with the belief that it would be of the greatest advantage to New Brunswick. If the fruits of confederation have not yet all been realized, that has been due rather to circumstances over which neither Mr. Tilley nor any one else had any control, than to any inherent vice of confederation itself. If union is strength, then it must be admitted that the union of the British North American provinces, which consolidated them into a powerful whole, was a good thing; and there cannot be a doubt that if the provinces had remained separate from each other, their present position would have been much less favourable than it is now.

[253]

CHAPTER X
THE BRITISH NORTH AMERICA ACT

One of the great objects of confederation was the construction of the Intercolonial Railway from St. John and Halifax to Quebec. It was thought that there could be no real union between the several colonies of British North America unless a good means of communication existed, and such a means was to be obtained only through the construction of this line of railway. The Intercolonial Railway, as we have seen, had been a part of the policy of successive governments in the province for many years, and it became an essential part of the scheme of confederation. When confederation was accepted by the people of New Brunswick in 1866, the Intercolonial Railway had yet to be built. Western Extension, as the line to the Maine border was called, had only been commenced; Eastern Extension, from the Shediac line towards Halifax, was in the same condition; in fact, the total mileage of the railways in New Brunswick did not exceed two hundred miles, and these lines were isolated and formed no part of any complete system. New Brunswick now has three separate lines of railway leading to Quebec and Montreal; it is connected with the great railway systems of the continent; [254] there is no county in the province which has not a line of railway traversing it; and the mileage has risen from less than two hundred to more than fourteen hundred.

Mr. Tilley realized that the time had come when the communities which form the British provinces of North America must either become politically connected or else fall, one by one, beneath the influence of the United States. After confederation had been brought about between Canada, New Brunswick and Nova Scotia, enough was seen in the conduct of American statesmen towards Prince Edward Island to show that their design was to try to create a separate interest in this colony apart from the general interest of Canada. The acceptance of the scheme of confederation by Prince Edward Island, at a comparatively early period, put an end to the plots in that quarter; but in the case of Newfoundland the same thing has been repeated, and an attempt was made by American statesmen to cause the people of that island to believe that their interests and those of Canada are not identical, and that they would be specially favoured by the United States if they held aloof from the great Dominion. The attitude of the people and congress of the United States towards Canada has not been marked, for the most part, by any great friendliness. They saw in confederation an arrangement that was likely to prevent this country from ever becoming absorbed by their [255] own, and they believed that by creating difficulties for us with respect to the tariff and other matters, and limiting the area of our commercial relations, they could put such pressure upon Canada as would compel our people to unite with them. This scheme has failed because it was based on a misconception of the spirit of our people; but who will say that it would not have succeeded if the several provinces which now form the confederation had been disunited and inharmonious in their relations and had pursued different lines of policy?

HIS SPEECHES

It is unfortunate that, owing to the absence of verbatim reports, it is impossible to reproduce any of Tilley's speeches during the confederation campaign. No speaker that New Brunswick has ever produced has been more generally acceptable than was Tilley. His speeches were pointed, and so clear that they could not be misunderstood. He possessed, to a very large extent, that magnetism which enabled him to retain the attention and to awaken the sympathy of his audience. At all the meetings which he addressed, there were many who regarded themselves always as his friends and supporters and who formed a phalanx around him, giving him a confidence and political strength which few statesmen have ever enjoyed to a like extent. Although his addresses frequently provoked the bitter animosity of his enemies, he had always enough friends to counteract their influence; and during the many contests which he had to fight [256] for his seat in the city of St. John, he was always able to rely on the loyalty of those who were his early associates and who remained his supporters until the end of his career. It is quite safe to assert that confederation could not have been carried had it not been for the personal efforts of Mr. Tilley. As the leader of the government which had consented to the Quebec scheme, he was properly looked upon as the chief promoter of confederation in New Brunswick, and his name will go down to future generations identified with that large and necessary measure of colonial statesmanship.

THE LEGISLATURE MEETS

Although the vote of the electors had been taken on the question, much remained to be done before confederation could become an accomplished fact. The last elections, which were those of Kings and Charlotte, were held on June 12th, but more than a year was to elapse before the union was effected, and the result which the election was intended to bring about realized. The first thing to be done was to call the legislature together and complete the business of the province, which had been interrupted by the dissolution. The legislature met on June 21st, and the Hon. John H. Gray, who had been an active advocate of confederation, and who was one of the members for the county of St. John, was made Speaker. In the speech from the throne the following reference was made to the question of confederation: [257] —

"Her Majesty's government have already expressed their strong and deliberate opinion that the union of the British North American provinces under one government is an object much to be desired. The legislatures of Canada and Nova Scotia have formed the same judgment, and you will now shortly be invited to express your concurrence with or dissent from the view taken of this great question by those provinces."

The address in reply was moved by Mr. Kerr, of Northumberland, and seconded by Mr. Beveridge of Victoria, and its consideration was made the order of the day for the following Saturday. When it came up for discussion the Hon. Albert J. Smith was not in his place, and Mr. Botsford, one of his colleagues from Westmorland, endeavoured to have the consideration of the matter postponed; but the House was in no humour to await the convenience of any single member, and the address was passed the same day by a vote of thirty to seven. Attorney-General Fisher, immediately on the passage of the address, gave notice of the following resolution, which was to be made the order of the day for Monday, June 26th: —

"*Resolved*, That an humble address be presented to His Excellency, the lieutenant-governor, praying that His Excellency be pleased to

appoint delegates to unite with delegates from the other provinces
in arranging with the imperial government for the union of British
North America, upon [258] such terms as will secure the just rights
and interests of New Brunswick, accompanied with provision for
the immediate construction of the Intercolonial Railway; each province to have an equal voice in such delegation, Upper and Lower
Canada to be considered as separate provinces."

Mr. Fisher moved the resolution in question in a very brief
speech, and was replied to by the Hon. Mr. Smith, who spoke at
great length and continued his speech on the following day. Mr.
Smith took exception to giving the delegates power to fix the destinies of the provinces forever, without again submitting the scheme
of union to the people. He proceeded to discuss the Quebec scheme,
and took exception to the construction of the Upper House of the
proposed legislature of the confederation, declaring that each province should have an equal number of representatives in it, as was
the case in the United States. After going over the ground pretty
thoroughly and criticizing most of the terms of the scheme of confederation, he moved an amendment, to the effect that no Act or
measure for a union with Canada take effect until approved by the
legislature or the people of the province.

A PLAN FOR CONFEDERATION

The Hon. Mr. Tilley replied to the leader of the Opposition in one
of the most effective speeches that he ever delivered in the legislature. He first took up Mr. Smith's allusion to the constitutional question, and, with immense power and solemnity, he charged that any
want of constitutional action [259] which existed was due to Mr.
Smith and his colleagues. He stated that the governor's sympathies
were with the late government, and that he had endeavoured to aid
and not to injure them. Mr. Smith had alluded to the Hon. Joseph
Howe, who was then an opponent of confederation, in terms of
praise, and Mr. Tilley, in reply, read from Mr. Howe's speech, made
in 1861, a magnificent paragraph on the union of British America.
Mr. Tilley stated that the government would take the Quebec
scheme for a basis, and would seek concessions to meet the views of
those who found objection to parts of it. He mentioned the various
counties of the province to show that they were either expressly or

potentially favourable to the Quebec scheme. He was convinced that even his friend, the ex-attorney-general and member for West-morland, was hardly against union. He asked, "Was there one anti-unionist on the floor of the House? Where was Mr. Anglin? Mr. Needham? Mr. Hill and all the rest of the anti-unionists? They were all swept away and unionists had taken their places, and when the arrangements for union were carried out, the feeling in its favour would be deeper and deeper." Mr. Tilley showed the great advantages which would accrue to New Brunswick eventually in consequence of confederation. He combated the statement made by Mr. Smith that after confederation the provincial legislature would become a mere farce, showing that of all the Acts passed [260] during the previous two years there were only seven which would have come under the control of the general legislature. Mr. Tilley closed by dwelling on the impression of power which union would have on the minds of those abroad who were plotting our ruin. The speech was listened to with the utmost attention by the members of the legislature and by a very large audience which completely filled the galleries, and it was generally considered to have been one of his greatest efforts.

SMITH'S AMENDMENT

The resolution was finally carried by a vote of thirty to eight, only two members, both of whom would have voted for the resolution, being absent. As soon as the confederation resolution was passed the Hon. A. J. Smith moved a resolution which, after reciting the steps which had already been taken in favour of union with Canada, continued as follows: —

"Therefore, *Resolved*, as the deliberate opinion of this House, that no measure for such union should be adopted which does not contain the following provisions, viz.: first, an equal number of legislative councillors for each province; second, such legislative councillors to be required to reside in the province which they represent and for which they are appointed; third, the number of representatives in the federal parliament to be limited; fourth, the establishment of a court for the determination of questions and disputes that may arise between the federal and local governments as to [261] the meaning of the Act of Union; fifth, exemption of this province from taxation for the construction and enlargement of canals in Upper Canada, and for the payment of money for the mines and minerals and lands of Newfoundland; sixth, eighty cents per head to be on the population as it increases and not to be confined to the census of 1861; seventh, securing to each of the Maritime Provinces the right to have at least one executive councillor in the federal government; eighth, the commencing of the Intercolonial Railway before the right shall exist to increase taxation upon the people of the province."

Mr. Smith supported his resolution in a lengthy speech in which he predicted increased taxation as the result of confederation. He said that the House, instead of being a deliberative assembly, had to surrender its judgment to the government. Confederation was a great experiment at best, and called for the exercise of other men's judgment. The government were going on in the most highhanded manner and were not justified in withholding information asked for. He elaborated the idea that Canada was pledged to issue treasury notes to pay present liabilities, and asserted that the government was altogether under the control of Canadian politicians. He insisted particularly on a provision in the Act of Union that each of the Maritime Provinces have an executive councillor in the federal government. Finally the vote was taken and the [262] following amendment, which had been moved by the Hon. Mr. Fisher, was carried, only eight members voting against it: —

"*Resolved*, That the people of this province having, after due deliberation, determined that the union of British North America was desirable, and the House having agreed to request His Excellency the lieutenant-governor to appoint delegates for the purpose of considering the plan of union upon such terms as will secure the just rights of New Brunswick, and having confidence that the action of His Excellency under the advice of his constitutional advisers will be directed to the attainment of that end, sound policy and a due regard to the interests of this province require that the responsibility of such action should be left unfettered by an expression of opinion other than what has already been given by the people and their representatives."

This ended the battle for confederation in New Brunswick, for what remained to be done was merely the arrangement of the details of the union by the delegates who had received full powers for that purpose. The session of the legislature, which must be considered one of the most important ever held in New Brunswick, came to a close on Monday, July 7th. At a meeting of the government held immediately after the prorogation, the Hon. Messrs. Tilley, Wilmot, Fisher, Mitchell, Johnson and Chandler were appointed to go to England as delegates for the purpose of meeting delegates from [263] Canada and Nova Scotia, and framing the bill which was to be passed by the imperial parliament for the consummation of confederation. It was understood that there would be no delay on the part of the delegates from Canada, but Sir John A. Macdonald and the other Canadian delegates were unable to leave at the time appointed, and did not meet the Maritime Provinces delegation in England until many months after the latter had arrived there. This unfortunate circumstance produced much comment at the time, because it looked as if the government of Canada was treating the delegates of New Brunswick and Nova Scotia with discourtesy. Instead of the business being completed promptly, as was expected, and the bill passed by the parliament during the autumn season, the whole matter was thrown over until the following year, and the New Brunswick delegates, most of whom were prominent members of the government, had to remain in England for about ten months at great expense and inconvenience.

THE DELEGATES IN ENGLAND

The delegates from the three provinces, Canada, Nova Scotia and New Brunswick, met at the Westminster Palace Hotel, London, in December, 1866, the Hon. John A. Macdonald in the chair and Lieut.-Col. Hewitt Bernard acting as secretary. The resolution passed at the Quebec conference held in 1864 was read, and amendments were moved in accordance with the suggestions made in the several legislatures during the discussions at the previous [264] sessions. It was conceded by all that the Intercolonial Railway, by which facilities for interprovincial commercial intercourse should be secured, must be built by the united provinces and without delay. It was also conceded that in the provinces where separate schools were established by law, that principle should not be disturbed. In the discussion it was claimed that the sole right of imposing an export duty should be vested in the federal authority. This was objected to by the New Brunswick delegates, on the ground that as the people of that province had expended a large sum of money in the improving of the navigation of the upper St. John, they had to recoup themselves by imposing an export duty on lumber shipped from the province. A considerable portion of the income thus received was paid by the lumbermen of the state of Maine, the advantage derived by them from such improvements being very great. The claim thus presented by the New Brunswick delegates was conceded, and the province was permitted to retain the right. This right was abandoned after confederation, the Dominion paying therefor a hundred and fifty thousand dollars per annum to the New Brunswick government.

THE BRITISH NORTH AMERICA ACT

During the sitting of the delegates, which lasted for two months, many conferences were held with Lord Carnarvon, then secretary of state for the colonies, and the law officers of the Crown, in regard to objections which were taken to some of the resolutions [265] adopted by the delegates. The governor-general of Canada, Viscount Monck, was in London at the time, and was able to render valuable assistance during the conference, owing to his intimate knowledge of the previous negotiations at Quebec. The arrangements there made, in regard to the strengthening of the central government, founded on the experience of the United States during the War of Secession, were adhered to in the London resolutions and accepted by the imperial authorities. When the bill reached parliament some amendments were suggested, but when it was pointed out that the bill as presented was the result of the most careful consideration of both the imperial authorities and the colonial representatives, the suggested amendments were not pressed and the measure passed through both Houses with very little discussion. But one spirit seemed to animate both the imperial government and the members of parliament, and that was to give the provinces interested the fullest powers consistent with their relation to the Empire. The parliamentary opposition to the measure was much less than might have been expected, when it is remembered that the opponents of confederation had representatives in London, well able to present objections from their standpoint, who had the ear of Mr. Bright and other members of the House of Commons. Her Majesty took a deep interest in the measure and expressed that interest to members of [266] the delegation, adding that she felt a great affection for her loyal Canadian subjects. While the bill was before the House of Lords, Messrs. Macdonald, Cartier, Galt, Tupper and Tilley were honoured by a private presentation to Her Majesty, at Buckingham Palace, and shortly afterwards all the members of the conference were presented at a drawing-room at the same place.

COUNTY COURT ACT

The New Brunswick delegates returned to Canada in the spring of 1867, having completed their labours, and the legislature was called together on May 8th. The business before it was of great importance, for the province was entering upon a new era as a member of the Canadian confederation, and the legislature was about to lose that portion of its powers which was delegated to the federal parliament. It is not, however, necessary to enter into any details of the work of the session, which was carried through without any particular difficulty, the Opposition being too weak to oppose seriously the measures of the government. It was felt on all sides that, as twelve members of the legislative council were about to become members of the senate of Canada, and as fifteen representatives were to be elected to the House of Commons, most of whom would come from the House of Assembly, a striking change would take place in the composition of the legislature, which would be deprived of the services of a large number of its ablest men. One of the important bills of the session was the passage [267] of the Act establishing county courts in the province, and in respect to this measure a difference of opinion took place between Mr. John M. Johnson, one of the delegates and member for Northumberland, and his fellow delegates to England. He thought that the legislature had no authority under the terms of confederation, or from any understanding between the delegates while in England, to create county courts, while the other delegates held a different view. The Act was passed, however, and has proved to be one of the most useful ever placed upon the statute-book, relieving the supreme court of many cases, both civil and criminal, which would otherwise block its business, and enabling them to be disposed of more rapidly than before. The county court judges appointed under this Act were, with one exception, taken from the legislature, and this made another serious drain upon its experienced members.

[269]

CHAPTER XI
THE FIRST PARLIAMENT OF CANADA

The British North America Act, by which the provinces of Upper and Lower Canada, New Brunswick and Nova Scotia were bound into a confederation, came into force by royal proclamation on the first day of July, 1867. When it is considered how vast and vital a change this measure brought about, it is surprising that it produced so little excitement anywhere. With the exception of one or two demonstrations which were made with flags by persons hostile to confederation, it was received in the province of New Brunswick, which had been so much excited during two elections, with perfect calmness, and although for some years afterwards there were always a number of persons opposed to union who predicted direful things from confederation, and thought it must finally be dissolved, the voices of such persons were eventually silenced either by death or by their acquiescence in the situation. To-day it may be safely declared that the Canadian confederation stands upon as secure a foundation as any other government in the civilized world.

In June, 1867, the Hon. John A. Macdonald, the leading spirit in the government of Canada, was [270] entrusted by Lord Monck, then governor-general, with the formation of a ministry for the Dominion. Mr. Macdonald naturally experienced a good deal of difficulty in making his arrangements. In the formation of the first ministry much care was necessary; provincial and national interests were to be thought of and denominational claims had to receive some attention. But the greatest difficulty arose with respect to old party lines. Mr. Macdonald thought that these ought, as far as possible, to be ignored, and accordingly selected his men from the leading advocates of confederation belonging to both parties, placing in his cabinet seven Conservatives and six Liberals. The Liberals included the names of Mr. W. P. Rowland and Mr. William MacDougall for Ontario. A large number of the Liberals of Ontario, including George Brown and Alexander Mackenzie, opposed this arrangement, called a public meeting in Toronto, and passed resolutions in favour of a strictly party government on the old lines. It declared hostility to the proposal for a coalition, and resolved to oppose Messrs. Rowland and MacDougall, should they accept office under Mr. Macdonald. This decision was carried out, but these gentlemen were both elected by good majorities. In this first ministry there were five members from Ontario, four from Quebec, two from Nova Scotia, and two from New Brunswick: S. L. Tilley and Peter Mitchell. [271]

The wisdom of the course adopted will be apparent when it is remembered that the question of confederation was not settled or carried on party lines, some of the Conservatives opposing and some Liberals supporting it. This was clearly the case in New Brunswick, as shown by the last two elections held there. About one-third of the Liberal party, and a like proportion of the Conservative party, opposed confederation at the second election. To have formed the first government on a party basis would have necessitated the selection of some men who were opposed to the union, and whose efforts might not have been devoted to making it a success.

FIRST CONFEDERATION MINISTRY

The first confederation ministry was a very strong one. The Hon. John A. Macdonald became premier and minister of justice; the Hon. George E. Cartier was minister of militia and defence; Alexander T. Galt was minister of finance; the Hon. William MacDougall was minister of public works; the Hon. W. P. Rowland was minister of inland revenue; the Hon. A. J. F. Blair, president of the privy council; the Hon. Alexander Campbell, postmaster-general; the Hon. J. C. Chapais, minister of agriculture; the Hon. Hector L. Langevin, secretary of state. The Hon. Mr. Tilley became minister of customs and the Hon. Mr. Mitchell minister of marine and fisheries, while the two Nova Scotia representatives, Messrs. Archibald and Kenny, became respectively secretary of state for the provinces and receiver-general. [272]

It will thus be seen that the Maritime Provinces had four representatives out of thirteen members of the cabinet, and this proportion has generally been maintained since that time; so that the fears of those who anticipated that the provinces by the sea would not receive fair treatment in the distribution of high offices have proved to be groundless. On the contrary, it can be said that the Maritime

Province members of the government appear always to have occupied a very influential position.

The office of minister of customs, which Mr. Tilley received, was thought by some of his friends to be less important than he deserved, they being of the opinion that he should have been made minister of finance. This office, however, went to Mr. Galt, who, owing to a difference with the rest of the government, resigned four months later, his place in the cabinet being taken by Sir John Rose, who held the office of finance minister until October, 1869, Sir Francis Hincks then receiving the appointment. It was not until the resignation of the latter in February, 1873, that Mr. Tilley became minister of finance. The office at first assigned to him, however, was one of great importance, involving as it did the reorganization of the entire establishment of the customs of Canada, and it gave ample scope for his great ability as a business man.

The elections for the House of Commons in the new parliament of Canada took place in August, [273] when Tilley was chosen to represent the city of St. John, and John H. Gray, the county. It had been expected, in view of the fact that these men had been so largely instrumental in bringing about confederation, that they would be allowed to walk over the course unopposed. This was the case with Mr. Gray, whose candidature met with no opposition; but Mr. Tilley was opposed by Mr. John Wilson, who received a very small vote. This needless and futile opposition to the candidature of a man who deserved so well from the province, was merely one of the proofs of the existence of political rancour in the breasts of those who had been defeated on the confederation question.

FIRST CANADIAN PARLIAMENT

The first parliament of united Canada met on November 6th, 1867, and the address was moved by the Hon. Charles Fisher, who had been elected to represent the county of York. The session was a very long one, lasting until May 22nd of the following year; but there was an adjournment, extending from December 21st to March 20th. This meeting of parliament was especially memorable, inasmuch as it brought together, for the first time, the representatives of all the provinces, and the ablest men of all political parties. The people of Ontario and Quebec were little known to the people of the

Maritime Provinces, and those who resided in the larger provinces in like manner knew comparatively little of their fellow-subjects who dwelt by the sea. It was expected by some [274] that the Maritime Province representatives would be completely overshadowed by men of greater political reputation belonging to the larger provinces, but this did not prove to be the case. The Maritime representatives at once took a leading position in parliament, and this position they have steadily maintained down to the present time. No man stood better in the House of Commons than the representative from St. John, the Hon. S. L. Tilley. At that time Her Majesty, the Queen, in acknowledgment of his services in the cause of confederation, had created him a Companion of the Bath, a distinction which was also given to the Hon. Charles Tupper, of Nova Scotia.

A vast amount of business had to be disposed of at the first session of the parliament of Canada. Although the Union Act embodied the plan upon which confederation was founded, it was necessary to supplement it by a great deal of special legislation, for the purpose of interpreting it and making preparations for the practical working of the constitution. In all the discussions relative to the measures which had to be passed at that time, Tilley took a prominent part, and, when the session was over, he had established in the House of Commons, as fully as he had in the legislature of New Brunswick, a reputation for ability as a speaker and as a man of affairs. He was looked upon as one whose wide knowledge of the needs of the province and whose experience in departmental work were [275] likely to be of the greatest use to the confederation. His high character gave weight at all times to his words, and caused him to be listened to with the most respectful attention. During the whole period that Tilley sat in the House of Commons, he had the pleasure of knowing that even his political enemies respected his character and abilities, and, with the exception of the premier, perhaps no man wielded a more potent influence in the councils of the Dominion than he.

It is not necessary here to trace to any large extent the career of Sir S. L. Tilley in the parliament of Canada; that belongs rather to the history of the Dominion than to a work which deals particularly with his connection with his native province. Only so much of his public life in the House of Commons will be dealt with as seems

188

necessary to complete his personal history. Tilley continued to hold the position of minister of customs during the whole of the term of the first parliament of Canada. This parliament held five sessions and dissolved in the summer of 1872, the general election being in the month of July, upon which occasion he was reëlected for the city of St. John without opposition.

MINISTER OF FINANCE

The second parliament met on March 5th, 1873. Eleven days before that time Mr. Tilley had become minister of finance, succeeding Sir Francis Hincks, who had resigned that office after holding it for more than three years. The advancement [276] of Mr. Tilley to this responsible and influential position was very pleasing to his friends, and was received with satisfaction by the country generally.

The first confederation ministry of Canada resigned office on November 5th, 1873, under circumstances which are a part of the political history of the Dominion and need not be gone into in this volume, further than to say that, whatever basis there may have been for charges of corruption in connection with the Pacific Railway contract against other persons in the government, none were ever preferred against Mr. Tilley; nor did any one suspect or believe that he had anything whatever to do with the transactions which led to the resignation of the government. Prior to that event Mr. Tilley had been appointed lieutenant-governor of the province of New Brunswick in succession to the Hon. Lemuel A. Wilmot, whose term had expired. Every one felt that the honour thus bestowed upon Tilley was a most fitting one, for he was New Brunswick's foremost son in political life, and had reached his high position purely through his own ability and his own good character. That position he filled a greater number of years than any of his successors are likely to do, and it is admitted on all sides that no man could have performed the duties of the office more satisfactorily than he did.

[277]

CHAPTER XII
FINANCE MINISTER AND GOVERNOR

Mr. Tilley took up his residence in the old Government House, Fredericton, and he must have been struck with the changed aspect of affairs from that presented under the old régime, when lieutenant-governors were appointed by the British government and sent out from England to preside over the councils of a people of whom they knew little or nothing. Most of these former governors had been military men, more accustomed to habits of command than to deal with perplexing questions of state. They looked with a very natural degree of impatience on the attempts which the people of the province were making to get the full control of their own affairs. Under the old régime the governor was surrounded with military guards, and sentries paced the walks and guarded the entrances to the Government House. The withdrawal of the British troops from Canada before the lieutenant-governorship of Mr. Tilley commenced relieved him of any embarrassment in regard to dispensing with military guards and sentries; but all pretentious accompaniments of authority were foreign to his nature, and he always showed, by the severe simplicity of his life, that he felt he was one [278] of the people, and that it was his duty as well as his pleasure to permit all who had any occasion to see him to have free access to him, without the necessity of going through any formal process.

THE PROTECTIONIST TARIFF

When Mr. Tilley became lieutenant-governor of the province, he was fifty-five years of age, and he seems to have thought that his political career was ended, because, by the time his term of office expired in its natural course, he would have reached the age of sixty, a period when a man is not likely to make a new entrance into public life. But circumstances, quite apart from any desire on his part, made it almost necessary for him to change his determination, and during the summer of 1878, when the general election was imminent, he found himself pressed by his old political friends to become once more the candidate of his party for his old constituency, the city of St. John. There was great enthusiasm amongst them when it was announced that he would comply with their wishes, and that he had resigned the lieutenant-governorship. The result of that general election is well known. The Liberal party, which had succeeded to the government less than five years before with a large majority in the House of Commons, experienced a severe defeat, and the Hon. Alexander Mackenzie, seeing this, very properly did not await the assembling of parliament, but sent in the resignation of the ministry, and Sir John A. Macdonald was called upon to form a new government. In the cabinet thus constructed Mr. [279] Tilley resumed his old office of minister of finance, and one of his first duties was to assist in the framing of a new customs tariff which was to give effect to the principle, upon which the election had been run, of protection to home industries. This idea of protection had not been heard of in the Canadian confederation as the policy of any political party until Sir John A. Macdonald took it up about a year before the general election, but it proved a winning card and was the means of giving the new government a long lease of power.

Sir Leonard Tilley's speech in introducing the new tariff was well received and made a strong impression upon all who heard it. It was admitted, even by those who were opposed to the views he held, that he showed a great mastery of the details, and that he illustrated in a very clear manner the view that the country was suffering because the duties imposed upon foreign goods were not sufficiently high to protect Canadian manufactures.

It is not the intention of this volume to deal to any full extent with the career of Sir Leonard Tilley during his second term of office as minister of finance of Canada. To enter into that phase of his career would be to relate the history of Canada, for he was but one member of the government, and not its leader. It is admitted that, in respect to financial questions, Sir Leonard showed the same ability that had characterized his career during his [280] previous term of office, and he was looked upon by his colleagues as a man in whose judgment the utmost confidence could be placed. At this time, however, his health began to fail, and the disease which finally carried him off developed to such an extent that he was told he must cease all active work or his days would be shortened. Under these circumstances, it became necessary for him to retire from the severe duties of his very responsible and laborious office, and on October 31st, 1885, he was again appointed lieutenant-governor of New

Brunswick, an office which he had filled with so much acceptance between 1873 and 1878. Sir Leonard Tilley continued lieutenant-governor during a second term, for almost eight years, or until the appointment of the Hon. John Boyd to that position. He was lieutenant-governor of New Brunswick for considerably more than twelve years, a record which is not likely to be equalled by any future lieutenant-governor for many years to come, if ever.

SECOND TERM AS GOVERNOR

There was no event of particular importance to distinguish Sir Leonard Tilley's second term as lieutenant-governor. The Hon. Mr. Blair was premier of New Brunswick during the whole period, and there was no political crisis of any importance to alter the complexion of affairs. The only event in connection with the governorship which is worthy of being mentioned is the change that was made by the abandonment of the old Government House, [281] at Fredericton, as the residence of the lieutenant-governor. This building had become antiquated, and in other ways unsuitable for the occupancy of a lieutenant-governor, and its maintenance involved a very large expenditure annually, which the province was unable to afford. It was therefore determined that in future the lieutenant-governor should provide his own residence, and that the amount spent on the Government House annually should be saved. Sir Leonard Tilley built a residence in St. John, in which he lived for the remainder of his life, and the seat of government, so far as his presence was concerned, was transferred to that city. Sir Leonard Tilley was always on the most cordial terms with the various premiers who led the government of New Brunswick during their terms of office. He knew well the strict constitutional limits of his office, and was always careful to confine his activities within their proper scope. The lessons of responsible government which he had learned in his early youth, and which had been the study of his manhood, enabled him to avoid those pitfalls which beset the steps of earlier lieutenant-governors.

During Sir Leonard Tilley's last term of office, and after its close, he abstained wholly from any interference with public affairs in the Dominion, and although he still remained steadfastly attached to the Liberal-Conservative party, he gave no outward sign of his desire for their success. This neutral [282] position which he assumed in political matters had the effect of drawing towards him thousands of his fellow-countrymen who, in former years, had been accustomed to regard him with unfriendly feelings. They forgot the active political leader and saw before them only the aged governor, whose venerable figure and kindly face were so familiar at social or other gatherings, or whenever work was to be done for any good cause. In this way Sir Leonard Tilley grew to assume a new character in the public estimation, and at the time of his death the regret was as great on the part of those who had been his political opponents as among those who had been his associates in political warfare. This was one of the most pleasing features of his declining years, and one that gave him the greatest satisfaction, because it enabled him to feel that he enjoyed the affectionate regard of the whole body of the people.

Sir Leonard Tilley throughout his life gave great attention to his religious duties. He was a devoted member of the Church of England, and his attendance at its services was constant and regular. For several years before his death he was connected with St. Mark's congregation, and no cause, except severe bodily illness, was ever allowed to prevent him from going to church on Sunday morning. On many occasions, when his steps had grown feeble and his strength was failing, it was suggested to him that he should drive to church, but he always replied [283] that he would walk to church as long as he had strength left to do so, and that he would not have people harnessing up horses on the Sabbath Day on his account. This resolution he maintained to the end of his life. Sometimes, when he met an old acquaintance, as he toiled up the street which led to his favourite church, he would cheerfully greet him by saying, "John, this hill has grown steeper than it used to be," but he climbed the hill to the end, and the last Sunday he was able to be out of his bed he walked to church as usual. He also took a deep interest in all humane and philanthropic objects as well as in the great work connected with the spread of the Gospel. He was a constant attendant at the annual meetings of the British and Foreign Bible Society, and was a life member of that admirable association.

HIS IMPERIAL HONOURS

The honours that Sir Leonard Tilley received from Her Majesty, in recognition of his great public services, were very gratifying to his friends as well as to himself, and when he was made a Knight Commander of St. Michael and St. George, in 1879, his temperance friends embraced the first opportunity on his return to St. John to have a banquet in his honour, at which he wore, for the first time in public, the insignia of the knightly order of which he had become a member. There was probably no public event in the whole course of his life which gave him greater pleasure than this proof of the attachment of his old friends. [284]

Sir Leonard's last visit to England was marked by an extremely gracious invitation to visit the queen at Osborne, in the Isle of Wight. While he and Lady Tilley were sojourning at Cowes a message was sent summoning them to Osborne House, where they were received by Her Majesty in the beautiful grounds that surround that palace. The Princess Louise and Princess Beatrice, with an equerry in waiting, were the only other persons present. After an interesting conversation they were permitted to visit the private apartments of Her Majesty, and the Prince Consort's farm.

Sir Leonard Tilley was first married in 1843 to Julia Ann, daughter of the late James T. Hanford, who died in 1862. By her he had seven children, two sons and five daughters. In 1867, he married Alice Starr, daughter of the late Z. Chipman, of St. Stephen. By this marriage he had two sons, Mr. Herbert C. Tilley, of the Imperial Trust Company, who resides in St. John, and Mr. L. P. DeWolfe Tilley, barrister, who is also a resident of St. John. These two sons, Herbert and Leonard, were the prop and comfort of his declining years and were devoted wholly to him to the end.

LADY TILLEY

Sir Leonard Tilley's second marriage was contracted at the time when he was exchanging the limited field of provincial politics for the wider sphere which confederation opened up to him in the parliament of Canada. It was a fortunate union, for it gave him a helpmeet and companion [285] who was in full sympathy with him in all his hopes and feelings, and who was singularly well qualified to preside over his household, which, in his capacity of a minister of the Crown, had become, to a considerable extent, a factor in the public life of Canada. Lady Tilley had a high ideal of her duty as the wife of a cabinet minister and of the governor of New Brunswick, and was not content to lead a merely ornamental life or confine her energies within a narrow range. She saw many deficiencies in our appliances for relieving human misery, and with a zeal which could not be dampened, she sought to remedy them. The Victoria Hospital at Fredericton is her work; hers also is the Nurses' Home in connection with the Public Hospital in St. John, and the Reformatory for the care of bad or neglected boys, who are in danger of becoming criminals if they are not educated and disciplined when they are young. In every work of philanthropy Lady Tilley has always taken not only an active, but a leading part, and her position has enabled her to enlist in the cause of humanity the energies of many who, under other circumstances, might not have given their attention to philanthropic work.

Sir Leonard Tilley for many years had suffered from an incurable disease, which had been mitigated by rest and medical treatment, but not removed. It was the knowledge of the fact that his days would be shortened if he continued in active political [286] life that compelled him to leave the government in 1885. For many years before his death the malady had been so far subdued that it gave him comparatively little trouble, but any unusual exertion on his part was almost certain to arouse it again to activity, so that he was prevented on many occasions from taking part in public functions which, under other circumstances, he would have been glad to attend. Still, he always contrived to take his daily walk, and few who saw him ever suspected that he was constantly menaced by death. For three or four years before his decease his strength had been failing, he stooped more as he walked, and it was evident that he was not destined to enjoy many more years of life. Yet during the spring of 1896 there was nothing whatever to indicate that the end was so near, for he went about as usual, and was able to preside at the annual meeting of the Loyalist Society which was held during the last week in May. On that evening he appeared very bright and cheerful, and he entered with much interest into the discussion of the details of an outing which it was proposed the society should hold during the summer. "Man proposes, God disposes." Sir Leonard had gone to Rothesay early in June to spend a few weeks in that pleasant spot, and he appeared to be in his usual health until the night of June 10th, when he began to suffer great pain from a slight cut which he had received in the foot. The symptoms became alarming and gave indications of [287] blood poisoning, a condition due to the disease from which he had suffered so many years. On June 11th, he was taken to Carleton House, his town residence, and from that time the doctors gave no hope of his recovery. It was one of the sad features of his illness that his life-long friend and physician for many years, Dr. William Bayard, was unable to attend him, being himself confined to his bed by illness.

LAST ILLNESS AND DEATH

After Sir Leonard Tilley reached his home in St. John he never rallied, and he was well aware that his end was near. He was attended by Dr. Inches and Dr. Murray McLaren, but he was beyond medical aid, and therefore the people of St. John, for several days before the event took place, were aware that their foremost citizen was dying. The time was one of great excitement, for the general election was near, yet the eyes of thousands were turned from the moving panorama of active life which passed before them to the silent chamber where the dying statesman was breathing his last. The regret and sympathy that was expressed was universal, and in their kindly words those who had been his life-long political opponents were not behind those who had been his friends. Sir Leonard Tilley died at three o'clock on the morning of June 25th, the second day after the general election which brought about the defeat of the party with which he had been so long identified. [288]

HIS EMINENT SERVICES

His death evoked expressions of sympathy and regret from all parts of the empire and from many states of the union. The letters and telegrams of condolence which Lady Tilley received during the first days of her widowhood would of themselves fill a volume, showing how widely he was known and respected. The funeral, which took place on the Saturday following his death, was one of the largest ever seen in St. John, and was attended by the Board of Trade, the Loyalist Society, the various temperance organizations, the members of the provincial government, and a vast concourse of prominent citizens. The services took place at St. John's Episcopal

Church, and were conducted by the rector, the Rev. John deSoyres, assisted by the Rev. R. P. McKim, rector of St. Luke's Church, with which Sir Leonard had been identified in his earlier years. The interment took place in the Rural Cemetery. Many references to the decease of this eminent man were made from the pulpits of St. John and other parts of the province on the Sunday following his death, and all the newspapers had long notices of the event and editorials on his life and character. We may fittingly close this work by quoting a portion of what was said of him by the St. John *Telegraph*, a paper that was politically opposed to him for many years: —

"It is greatly to the honour of Sir Leonard Tilley that no scandal, public or private, was ever attached to his name. A consistent temperance [289] man to the end of his life, he was faithful to the cause which he had espoused when he was young, and he enjoyed the confidence and received the steady support of a vast majority of the temperance men of the province, who looked upon him as their natural leader. His capacity for friendship was great, and his friends might be numbered by thousands, for he had a peculiar faculty of strongly attracting men to himself. This may be ascribed, in part, to the magnetism of a buoyant and strong nature, but it was more largely due to the extreme simplicity of his character, which remained wholly unspoiled by the favours which fortune had showered upon him. No man, however humble, had any difficulty in obtaining an interview with Sir Leonard Tilley; he was every inch a gentleman, and was, therefore, as polite to the poorest labourer as to the richest in the land. Such a man could not fail to be loved even by those who had been his most bitter opponents in former years, when he was in active political life.

"It is one of the drawbacks of this human life that the wise, the learned, the good, and those whom we most love and honour, grow old and feeble, fall by the wayside and pass away. So while we lament the death of Sir Leonard Tilley, we must recognize it as an event that was inevitable, and which could not long have been postponed. His lifework was done; his labours were ended; his active and brilliant career was closed; he was [290] but waiting for the dread summons which sooner or later must come to all. The summons has come, and he has gone from among us forever. His venerable, noble face will no longer be seen on our streets, his kindly greeting will no longer be heard. But his memory will live, not only in the hearts of all his countrymen, but enshrined in the history of this his native province, and of the great Dominion which he did so much to create, and which he so fondly loved."